DISCOVERY: HOW TO WIN YOUR CASE WITHOUT TRIAL

John A. DeMay

DISCOVERY: HOW TO WIN YOUR CASE WITHOUT TRIAL

Prentice-Hall, Inc.   Englewood Cliffs, New Jersey

Prentice-Hall International, Inc., *London*
Prentice-Hall of Australia, Pty. Ltd., *Sydney*
Prentice-Hall Canada, Inc., *Toronto*
Prentice-Hall of India Private Ltd., *New Delhi*
Prentice-Hall of Japan, Inc., *Tokyo*
Prentice-Hall of Southeast Asia Pte. Ltd., *Singapore*
Whitehall Books, Ltd., *Wellington, New Zealand*

"This publication is designed to provide accurate and authoritative information in regard to the subject matter covered. It is sold with the understanding that the publisher is not engaged in rendering legal, accounting, or other professional service. If legal advice or other expert assistance is required, the services of a competent professional person should be sought."

—*From the Declaration of Principles jointly adopted by a Committee of the American Bar Association and a Committee of Publishers and Associations.*

Library of Congress Cataloging in Publication Data

DeMay, John A.
  Discovery, how to win your case without trial.

  Includes index.
  1. Discovery (Law)—United States.   I. Title.
KF8900.D45   347.73'72   82-5239
                      347.30772   AACR2
ISBN 0-13-215640-7

Printed in the United States of America

ABOUT THE AUTHOR

John A. DeMay is in partnership with his son, Patrick J. DeMay, under the firm name of DeMay & DeMay, Attorneys at Law, in Pittsburgh, Pennsylvania. Since 1957, he has devoted himself principally to representing the Plaintiff's case, particularly in personal injury actions. A graduate of the University of Pittsburgh Law School, Order of the Coif, he was admitted to the Bar in 1953. He is a former Assistant United States Attorney for the Western District of Pennsylvania and is admitted to practice before the U.S. Supreme Court, the U.S. Court of Appeals, 2nd and 3rd Circuits, the U.S. District Court, Western Pennsylvania, the U.S. District Court for the Western District of New York, the U.S. District Court for the Northern District of Ohio, and all state courts in Pennsylvania. He is a member of the Academy of Trial Lawyers of Allegheny County, the American Trial Lawyers Association, and many other legal organizations.

DEDICATION

This book is dedicated to my wife, Helen Louise, who inspired me with the courage to attempt it, the tenacity to complete it, and whose threats to impose sanctions were a constant spur to good work. Her love of the Law and the understanding of the problems of trial lawyers are reflected in this book.

Foreword

No phase of the litigation process has received more critical comment in recent years than discovery. Opinions of the United States Supreme Court, as well as other courts, proposals by the Civil Procedural Rules Advisory Committee, and articles in legal journals all reflect growing disenchantment. What was originally expected to end trial by ambush and promote speedier, just resolution of law suits has instead led to complaints of harassment, delay, and unnecessary expense. Reports that discovery has been used as a weapon of attrition rather than a means of developing truth are widespread.

Although abuse of discovery may be intentional in some instances, a lack of skill in the art in many cases is at least as likely a cause. The practitioner who would increase his competence in this very important part of the litigation, however, has had surprisingly little in the way of text material to guide him. It is particularly fortunate, therefore, that John De May has chosen to devote his latest book to the very timely topic of discovery.

Mr. DeMay is a highly regarded trial lawyer who has drawn on his years of active practice in the courtroom to explain how discovery can be used effectively, not only in winning a verdict but also, and more often, to bring about a favorable settlement. He analyzes the relative advantages of interrogatories, depositions, and requests for admission, and suggests when each should be used. He writes candidly of the need to establish goals for discovery in each case so that the client's money, the lawyer's energy, and the court's time are not wasted.

Recognizing the growing belief that trial judges should become more active in a supervisory role, Mr. DeMay even suggests proper steps to pave the way to secure sanctions against recalcitrant adversaries. He writes in a readable and interesting style, frequently illustrating his points with instructive anecdotes from his extensive career at the trial bar, and making generous use of illustrative forms.

Many lawyers do not realize the value of discovery in bringing about an early and satisfactory disposition of a lawsuit. In an era of overcrowded dockets and inevitable delay in bringing a case to trial, effective discovery as a means to resolving factual issues is an alternative that Mr. DeMay argues persuasively.

I am confident that if the principles in this book were put into practice by the majority of the bar, much pretrial skirmishing would disappear and the aims of the original proponents of discovery would be met. Consequently, I have no hesitancy in saying that active trial lawyers will find the book to be valuable indeed. Those who enter the courts only occasionally should consider it as essential reading.

> Judge Joseph F. Weis, Jr.
> United States Court of
> Appeals for the Third
> Circuit

A Word from the Author

There is one good question that might well be asked of any Trial Lawyer, whether a Plaintiff's attorney or Defense counsel: when you take on a new case, do you give any thought to how you're going to win it? Probably not. If you are like most attorneys, you will have some vague concept of "trying the case"—someday; or some equally ill-defined notion that it "may settle"—eventually. How often have you heard your fellow-practitioners say that they are "waiting for the case to come to trial" or "hoping for a settlement," as though "waiting" and "hoping" were the roads to success. They're not.

This book is about winning cases—your cases, whether they involve Trespass, Assumpsit, Eminent Domain or a Will Contest. And it's about winning your case in one-half the time it will take for the case to come to trial. This book is about Discovery.

You probably think you know enough about discovery—depositions, interrogatories, and the like. You do know the words and you have used these legal tools from time to time, but the question is whether you have invoked discovery, wisely and well, *to win a case* rather than as a routine procedure. There is a vast difference between the two approaches, and unfortunately most attorneys invoke discovery with little zeal and no faith in its effectiveness. Let's face it: most lawyers—possibly even including yourself—look upon discovery as a drudge, a chore, more akin to digging a ditch than to practicing law. That's too bad. As many old-time Forty-Niners could attest, there is a lot of incentive to digging if there is a good possibility of uncovering gold. And that is what lies before you when you really work at discovery and know what you are doing.

This applies no matter which side of the case you are handling. If it is correct that many Plaintiff's attorneys are somewhat hesitant about admitting that they can win a case via Discovery, then it must be said that an equal number of Defense attorneys are absolute non-believers. And that's not right. In this book, we cite a concrete example of a good Defense

9

attorney winning a case by preparing an excellent set of Requests for Admissions followed by a Motion for Summary Judgment. The same thing has happened *often* (and illustrations are provided here) when a Plaintiff's or Defense attorney takes a good deposition of the opposing party, secures damning admissions, and follows up with a Summary Judgment Motion. It can be done! Defense attorneys can do a great job of either winning a case outright by the skillful use of Discovery or of devastating the Plaintiff's case so badly that a low settlement results.

Plaintiff's attorneys can do the same thing. If you are a Plaintiff's lawyer, just pause for a moment to think about your new case and you will soon realize that you don't know much about it. Your client has given you a biased, fragmentary and disjointed account of an event, or series of events, that occurred some time ago. Based on this information (hopefully supported by some investigation), you will prepare and file a Complaint. The Complaint isn't going to scare anyone. It is, in essence, a notice of suit accompanied by a statement of some facts (which you hope to be correct) and a theory of liability (which you may have conjured up out of the facts with crossed fingers and a muttered prayer).

Now what? Is any defendant going to come running to you to discuss settlement just because you filed a Complaint? Not at all. So what happens? You could do your usual thing and half-heartedly serve a Notice of Deposition on the principal defendant, prepare a few Interrogatories to get the names of witnesses, and let it go at that. Then you could set the file aside for a questionable result at some distant trial date. Or, after reading this book, you can buckle down for some hearty discovery that is going to win your case, and in much less time than it will take to get it to trial.

Look at a lawsuit from the defendant's point of view. The Complaint is nothing more than you intended it to be. The defendant knows that he is being sued, he disputes many of your facts, and he may be amused, intrigued or annoyed at your theory of liability. But he isn't going to panic and rush to pay you any money.

Now, suppose you follow up that Complaint with a well-constructed, detailed set of Interrogatories; then take several Depositions—not merely of the principal defendant but also of vital, peripheral witnesses; then serve a Motion to Produce very specific documents; and finally, nail down key facts with a Request for Admissions. Then watch the attitude of your opponent change. When you develop a case in this manner, the defendant begins to see that what began as a questionable case is evolving into a sure thing—for you. Thereafter, the correspondence between the Defense attorney and his client changes from "Is there any liability?" to "What are the damages and how much will we have to pay?"

That is exactly the position in which you want to place your opponent. When he begins to think like that, he is ready for the final step—serious settlement neogtiations.

That's the way to win a case.

You will be on your way to the bank with a substantial settlement check while your buddy across the hall twiddles his thumbs, his file still in a drawer gathering dust as he waits for that elusive and protracted "trial date."

Discovery is the key to success in every case. If yours is a good case, discovery will force opposing counsel to recognize that fact; if you have a poor case, discovery will help you to realize that you're not going anywhere with it and will enable you to avoid the expenditure of great quantities of time and money in a fruitless cause.

Finally, the proper use of discovery is an art—a talent that has to be developed. The first thing we want to discuss is your attitude toward it and the "atmosphere," if you will, in which you work. Those important matters are discussed in Chapter 1, followed promptly by a review of the principal discovery tools, the sequence in which to use them, and the ways of combining them with each other and with Motions. Subsequent chapters will explore in detail the intricacies of taking Depositions, preparing Interrogatories and Requests for Admissions, and Motions to Produce Documents. Finally, we will discuss in the concluding chapter how to effectively utilize the information you have gathered to bring about a happy settlement of your case.

The goal of every attorney is to conclude a case to the satisfaction of his or her client and himself or herself. For too long have you contemplated achieving the goal solely through a trial or a settlement at some indefinite date far in the future. You have the opportunity to force things to happen— to bring about prompt action on your case—without sitting and waiting. Above all, you have the means available to you to win your case in a expeditious manner. That means is called *Discovery,* and that is what this book is all about—winning through discovery—and doing so quickly. It takes time, effort, and some guidance. If you will take the time and exert the effort, this book will provide you with the guidance.

John A. DeMay

Table of Contents

Educate the client. Know your case well. Have an opinion and express it. Talk about a range of settlement, not a particular figure. Get the client commited—in writing.

Even questionable cases can be settled.

Verdicts set the standards for settlement. Settlements recently made by fellow lawyers are a reasonable guide. Utilize the various books and guides found in every law library.

Documentation of a plaintiff's claims. The current state of the law in novel cases. Letting your opponent have your items of proof as to liability. Evaluating a different case. Giving the other attorney the documentary information he needs.

Chapter 1

Strategy and Technique for Successful Discovery

DISCOVERY TODAY—A WHOLE NEW BALL GAME

A friend of mine—a prominent defense attorney—recently addressed a group of young lawyers on the subject of cross-examination. At one point he made the startling assertion: "Cross-examination is dead. Discovery killed it." I admit to choking a little on hearing that comment, having just lost a case based in good part on the devastating cross-examination of my client by opposing counsel. Of course my friend was emphasizing by exaggeration, but the thrust of his argument is sound. Prior to the post-World-War-II era there was very little discovery, and lawyers prepared their cases in deliberate isolation with a great emphasis placed on "hiding" facts, documents and even witnesses from the other side. As a result the first contact an attorney had to the facts known by his opponent was in the courtroom during the direct examination of a witness. In just a few moments he had to analyze that testimony and then attack it through cross-examination. Is it any wonder that the art of cross-examination was developed to a high degree and its successful practitioners greatly esteemed? They were functioning in a "now or never" situation. Lawyers of that era still talk of trying a lawsuit "by the seat of the pants"—much like the way the pilots of the time flew their fabric-covered biplanes. It must have been an exciting and dramatic way to handle a lawsuit and, of course, THE TRIAL was everything. Apparently, though, many thinking persons began to wonder whether the cause of justice was well served by this procedure and decided that the answer was "no." Cross-examination, as the sine qua non of trial, was seen as so subjective and personal an art, and skillful cross-examination so beyond the capability of many trial lawyers, that it was felt some other way had to be found to advance the cause of justice between disputing parties. Certainly the major change wrought by this reasoning was in the Discovery Rules incorporated in the new Federal Rules of Civil Procedure which came into being in 1946. They may have been technical rules, but they dramatically changed the whole attitude and approach of lawyers in the handling of lawsuits.

DISCOVERY EXISTS TO INFORM LAWYERS, SHORTEN TRIALS AND ENCOURAGE SETTLEMENTS

It might jokingly be said that the old-time lawsuit was made up of equal parts of stealth, subterfuge, and surprise. If this was so, the new discovery rules were expressly designed to completely reverse those attributes and to expose the entire preparatory process to fresh air and sunshine. Open disclosure became the name of the game. The older lawyers may have been shocked, but under the prodding of a determined judiciary, they were required to identify witnesses, produce documents, and answer pointed questions about the conduct of their client; and the client was subjected to intensive interrogation by the process of deposition.

The thought behind the changes was that through a policy of open disclosure each party to a dispute could learn in detail all the facts concerning it, and then could analyze these facts at leisure. In this way, it was hoped, lawyer and client could view their position more intelligently, and settlement would necessarily result. (Of course, this presumed a certain degree of good faith and a willingness to face the facts developed by discovery—two qualities that are often lacking in litigants, be they irate individuals or bureaucratic corporations.) In addition, it was thought, if the parties could not settle their dispute, thorough discovery would certainly reduce the time of trial itself. Since each side would know the details of the other's case there could be stipulations, a waiver of proof as to documents, fewer witnesses and shorter cross-examination.

To the credit of the originators of these ideas, things have pretty much worked out the way they had hoped. In the jurisdiction in which I practice, fully 80 percent of the cases are settled prior to trial and the trial of a routine negligence or assumpsit case rarely takes more than three to five days.

GETTING ALL THE FACTS

It is rare to find a case in which the issues are exclusively legal ones. Can you remember the last time you sat down with your opponent, stipulated every fact involved in a case, and then presented it to the Court for determination as a pure question of law? We call that a Case Stated. I have a vague memory of having done that once a long time ago, but it is such a rarity that I have long since dismissed it from my mind. Almost by definition lawsuits involve factual disputes. To be sure, legal issues arise in interpreting the facts, but disputed facts are the first matter that requires resolution in a trial. The problem of who said what is usually the issue in a contract dispute, and the problem of who did what is at the heart of every negligence case. The answers to these questions lie in the facts known, or believed, by each party and the surrounding witnesses. Discovery enables the attorney to learn these facts. With them he can sensibly decide what kind of case he has; without them he is blind and has no idea where he is going. That important difference is more than enough to justify the discovery rules and the devotion of serious effort to utilizing them.

In addition, there is another virtue in Discovery, and it arises because of the honest ignorance of one's client.

YOUR CLIENT KNOWS ONLY SOME OF THE FACTS—YOUR OPPONENT KNOWS THE REST

Too often, attorneys proceed on these two false assumptions:

1. Their client knows the facts and can tell them all they need to know; and,
2. Their client tells the truth, the whole truth and nothing but the truth.

In the vernacular—and bluntly put— "It just ain't so!"

Every experienced attorney knows this; the inexperienced ones should learn it promptly. The tale is often told—and constantly bears repeating— about the psychology teacher who stages a disruption in his classroom with two boys rushing in, shouting and fighting, and then running out of the room. Then he asks the class to write a report describing the event and the participants. Amazingly, if he has 25 students, he will get 25 variations of who, what, where and when. Our powers of observation and recollection are simply not acute enough, or properly developed enough, to enable us to report exactly what happened. How much more difficult it is when we are personally involved—in an accident, for example, where things happen very quickly, or in a Will Contest among family members where emotionalism runs rampant.

Let's face it—your client doesn't know all the facts and even the ones he or she claims to know are often distorted by self-interest, anger, vindictiveness, or an honest desire to explain that it simply "must have been that way."

Your opponent knows many facts that your client doesn't know. Even in such an elemental matter as the names of witnesses, he knows things that your client doesn't know. In addition, he may have been in a better position to observe facts, he may have more ready access to documents, and he may simply have a better memory than your client. To illustrate: who knows most about what happened during an operation—the patient or the surgeon?

Happily one need not rely solely on one's client. Because of the discovery rules you can expand your knowledge to include everything the other side knows or believes. These rules enable you to fill in the gaps in your own knowledge of what happened, and also enable you to get the attitude, opinions and views of your opposing litigant regarding those facts. That later can be just as important as the facts.

THE WEAPONS IN YOUR DISCOVERY ARMORY

There are four major tools available to you for the purpose of gathering information from your adversary. They are described here:

1. Interrogatories: A series of questions that must be answered under oath. Those questions need not relate directly to the subject matter of the lawsuit, although as a matter of generality and common sense they will. One is permitted to ask questions which can lead to information that relates to the subject matter of the case.

2. Requests for Admission: A series of statements of fact which the other side must admit or deny under oath. This procedure has value in clearing the air of facts that are necessary to prove and that the other side has no interest in contesting. They are easily evaded because so much depends on the precision of the wording.

3. Motion to Produce Documents: A procedure designed to permit one to secure, inspect and copy written material in the possession or control of your opponent. This is an invaluable tool.

4. Depositions: A procedure in which one compels a party or witness to appear and, under oath, submit to a verbal examination concerning any matter relevant to the lawsuit. Probably this is the most widely used discovery tool, and it is highly effective if the attorney is properly prepared and knows what he's after. While this technique is nearly always utilized by attorneys, it is not often utilized wisely and well.

There are some miscellaneous techniques that are available for specific purposes. Thus, for example, a defendant in a personal injury action can compel an injured plaintiff to submit to a physical examination. There is a procedure whereby one can take a deposition by written interrogatories. These are not used often and need only be touched upon in this book.

DEFINE THE ISSUES! A LEGAL IMPERATIVE

The call has been repeated over and over again from the first day of law school: "Define the issues!" That is just as important in discovery as it is in any other aspect of a lawsuit. Without a clear understanding of the issues your discovery will proceed in a willy-nilly fashion, without rhyme or reason, and will result in your collecting information that is not pertinent to the issues and your spending a lot of time gathering useless facts. If, in an Assumpsit action, the issue is when and where a party mailed his acceptance of an offer, why spend a lot of time on discovery about the consideration supporting the contract? In a slander action the central issue may well be the identity of the precise words used; why go to great lengths inquiring about the time, place and circumstances of the usage? This is what I mean about identifying the issues. Know what you want and need— then spend your time achieving this goal.

RESEARCH THE APPLICABLE LAW

With the facts your client can give you, you have a fair idea of what happened and a reasonable appreciation of the issues. But, before you start running off to dictate interrogatories or schedule a deposition, take time to do some research on the applicable law. It could well be that your general knowledge has some important gaps in it, that the statutory law has changed since the last time you handled a case such as this, or that there have been recent court opinions emphasizing the need for additional proof of some element of liability or damages that exists in your case. Such research can't take much time, and that time will be well spent. First of all it insures that you aren't overlooking a significant aspect of your case and, second, it enables you to frame your discovery so as to pinpoint a matter that you have to prove. As we all know, the law is a vibrant and lively subject, and a few minutes in a library will help you to be certain that you have a clear idea concerning matters that you have to prove.

HAVE A SPECIFIC GOAL IN MIND

There's more to this than merely saving time, although we are certainly all concerned with that subject. It's also a matter of purpose or intent. Why are you serving Interrogatories? What documents do you want from the defendant? What admissions do you want him to make? Whether you call it a purpose or a goal, you must have some clear-cut idea of what you are after when you proceed with discovery. Defining the issues is a great help; thereafter you should plan just what facts you need to win your case and then decide on the appropriate discovery tool to gather this information. The whole idea is to concentrate your efforts on gathering the precise data you need rather than proceeding with discovery indiscriminately.

MIX AND MATCH—USE ALL THE AVAILABLE TOOLS

There is no rule that restricts you to any one type of discovery; they are all available to you. Use them. In addition, there is no law that says you can use them only once and then not again. Use them often—and mix them up. Suppose you start with Interrogatories and then learn that certain documents you need are in the possession of your opponent. Go ahead and serve a Request for Production of Documents. But after you have received and reviewed the documents you may very well find they have raised additional questions in your mind. That's fine; get the answers by serving additional Interrogatories. With background material securely in hand, go ahead with a deposition of a party or witness. You may learn that someone else has documents that sound interesting. You can get them by preparing another Request for Production. Finally, to establish the validity of some of the documents and to avoid proof in Court of some essential but non-disputed facts, serve a Request for Admissions. In other words, use all your discovery tools and mix them up as needed.

DON'T ABUSE DISCOVERY

At the time of this writing there is a serious effort being made to reform the Federal discovery rules. They have been abused. A deposition that should take one afternoon is stretched out to a full week; instead of serving 30 specific interrogatories an attorney will serve 150, 90 percent of which are really irrelevant but just enough within the rules to make it necessary to answer them. A corporation will be asked to produce enormous quantities of documents that may span a decade, well knowing that the requesting party will use a mere handful of them and may not even look at the majority of them.

This is unfortunate, and it is my observation that it is principally a fault of the major law firms in each city. They are the only ones with clients who are willing to pay for endless hours spent on this foolishness. The sole practitioner who has a case on a contingent fee basis and the small law firm whose insurance-company client watches the bills like a hawk simply cannot afford the time for what is essentially unnecessary and unjustifiable discovery. It is in their interest to get to the heart of the matter quickly at the least cost to their client and with as little expenditure of time as possible.

By way of example let me refer to that deposition that lasted a week. The lawsuit was against a major corporation which was represented by a large law firm. I deposed four corporate officers in one afternoon. I knew exactly what I wanted and got it, promptly and concisely. The deposition of my client lasted a week. Why? In essence the deposition covered his entire life—the jobs he held, why he left them, arguments with his superiors, who said what and when, his military career—nothing was left out. The Transcript is so voluminous that it is painful to look at. From those hundreds of pages of transcript there aren't more than 150-200 that have any utility. The rest is biography and sociology. Interesting, but with no genuine relevance to the issues involved in the lawsuit. About the only way it could be justified is on the theory that *every* event in a person's life could *possibly* become relevant in a trial.

That's true, but it's not a good enough reason to go to such lengths in discovery. It does do one thing, though—it earns a substantial income for the law firm.

In my opinion this is an abuse of discovery. Because of many instances like this we may get substantial restrictions on discovery in the future.

In any event, don't do it. Use discovery as a rapier, not as a broadsword. Pick and choose what you need, then go get it. Know the issues, decide the facts you need to resolve them, then choose the discovery procedure that will help you to gather those precise facts. Nothing more is needed. There is such a thing as overkill in discovery just as there is in nuclear weaponry.

DISCOVERY AND INVESTIGATION ARE PARTNERS— NOT COMPETITORS

Discovery will never take the place of investigation. It will supplement investigation and help you to limit the extent and scope of your investigation, thereby saving you some money, but it will never replace investigation. There are certain times, however, and they occur frequently, when an investigator cannot gather the information you need. A manufacturing company, or a hospital, will not open its files to an investigator, but it will do so in response to an Order of Court. A person may refuse to talk to an investigator but can be compelled to come to your office and answer questions at a deposition. The two procedures—discovery and investigation—should work together, hand in hand, each accomplishing what the other cannot. In some cases an investigator may not even be able to start his work until you have secured the identity of witnesses by serving Interrogatories on your opposing counsel, and your architect-expert may need drawings that you will have to secure by a Motion to Produce. Discovery can never preempt the field of investigation; it can only supplement it.

BUILD A SOLID CASE—FOR SETTLEMENT, A SUMMARY JUDGMENT OR A QUICK AND EASY TRIAL

The whole purpose of discovery is to elicit facts from your opponent which, together with the ones that you already have, will enable you to win your case.

If you are very diligent and skillful, you may be able to gather enough admitted facts to enable you to get a Summary Judgment and avoid a trial entirely. Admittedly that is rare, but it does happen. More frequently you will gather sufficient evidence to convince your opponent that there is no hope of his winning the lawsuit and he will be very receptive to settlement negotiations.

Let me illustrate these statements by two examples:

In my jurisdiction we have the Doctrine of Informed Consent in medical malpractice actions. In a case involving surgery I deposed the defendant doctor and led him through the specific requirements of Informed Consent. We covered the "part of the body involved," "nature of the operation," and "alternatives to the operation," and he did just fine. Then we reached the part about "possible ill effects" of the operation. At this point he faltered and fell. I moved for a Summary Judgment and got it.

In a recent case against an insurance company which issued a disability insurance policy—and then refused to pay on the ground of a relation back to a "preexistent" condition—I deposed the underwriter, the claims man and the president. The more information I secured, the more I felt that a claim for punitive damages was in order. In a highly technical medical matter all the decisions were being made by persons who were completely untrained in medicine, and not one of them had even tried to get a medical opinion. When it became obvious that things were getting very bad, the insurance company suggested that a settlement was in order. I agreed.

These things just didn't happen—like lightning out of a clear blue sky. The end result was the product of hard work, deliberate planning, and discovery techniques that were carefully thought out and executed according to a definite outline—a written, prepared outline that was part of the file while the entire proceeding was going on.

Finally, if the case must be tried, your efforts in discovery can shorten your trial time—and isolate the remaining issues so that you can concentrate your talents on a few vital issues rather than worrying and proving a veritable host of important but miscellaneous matters.

Discovery can accomplish great things for you. Use it freely, but wisely.

Chapter 2

The Effective Use of Legal Assistants

No lawyer works on a case alone. Each of us solicits and receives some kind of help in the development and preparation of a lawsuit. Certainly the first line of support is our secretary, in whom we place a great deal of trust and confidence and, depending on his or her experience, to whom we can assign significant tasks in the discovery phase of a case. Frequently we have an associate attorney in our office who is assigned to work with us on a case, or a referring attorney who wants to participate. Finally, in today's world, the paralegal has become a standard fixture in many law offices. All of these persons can be of great help to you in the discovery process, but it does take some special effort on your part to utilize them effectively.

When assistants work with you there has to be organization of the work to be done and an understanding—a "modus operandi" if you will—as to how it is to be done. If either is ignored, the partnership breaks down very quickly and becomes quite ineffective.

This chapter explores the problems of how to work with others in discovery proceedings, and gives you some practical ideas on how to make the team perform efficiently and successfully.

In thinking about your discovery you must give some consideration to these factors:

1. Deciding what facts you need;
2. Determining which discovery technique best secures those facts;
3. Preparing the appropriate pleading;
4. Analyzing the answers or response; and
5. Deciding the additional data you need and how to get it.

In answering these questions you have to work closely with your assistant—explaining, supervising, criticizing and directing. These duties have problems of their own and they deserve a close look.

29

THE ROLE OF THE LEGAL ASSISTANT IN DISCOVERY PROCEDURES

It is good to remember that any aid and assistance you receive from others is designed to help you, not replace you. That is a distinction that lawyers ought to think about. Too many of them look upon their assistant as *the* person to take over all the hard work of preparation in a lawsuit. When these attorneys assign work they seem to proceed on the assumption that the secretary, paralegal, or associate attorney ought to know everything *they* know about the law and the case, and ought to be able to do everything *they* can do. (Naturally this presumption is never permitted to extend to such mundane matters as equal pay and equal rights around the office.) This attitude is unfortunate because it inevitably leads to a breakdown in a system that is supposed to work smoothly and to result in an increase in the effective productivity of an office. Note the key word "effective."

Most of the blame rests with the lawyer. He is in charge and gives the orders. Unless there is an out-and-out personality conflict, any reasonably trained person should be of great help to the lawyer, provided the attorney *takes the time to*

Explain the facts,
Outline the issues,
Discuss the law, and
Assign specific tasks.

I am certain that some reader will feel obliged to make the flippant comment: "If I do all of that, I might as well do the discovery work myself." That's not so, and the comment reveals hasty, ill-considered reasoning. It may require one hour of an attorney's time to carefully explain the things that have to be done—the kind of interrogatories you want, for example—but it may well take eight hours for the paralegal (or the attorney) to do the work. These same proportions, in time spent by the attorney and time saved for him, exist to one degree or another in all phases of discovery. The saving in time and effort on the part of the lawyer is very substantial, provided the assistant has a clear idea of just what he or she is supposed to do.

Essentially the choice must be made by you, the attorney! You can either explain carefully the work you want done and its purpose so that your assistant goes about the detailed work with understanding, or you can give abrupt and general instructions and permit your assistant to work in ignorance. One method results in a lot of good work; the other leads to ill feelings and a waste of time.

ASKING AND GETTING—MAKING YOUR NEEDS
UNDERSTANDABLE TO PRODUCE GOOD RESULTS

I pointed out earlier that a common problem of attorneys vis-à-vis their paralegal assistant is that they act as though the assistant knows as much as they do. Unfortunately, one's assistant is not one's clone or alter-ego. You simply cannot give the instruction, "Draw up interrogatories," and let it go at that. Your helper does not know the questions that might be specific for your factual situation as opposed to those that provide general background information; he or she cannot be expected to realize those facts that are legally necessary—an essential element of proof—in your case; and finally, the assistant cannot, in the abstract, appreciate what the central issues are so as to emphasize questions relating to these issues in the interrogatories. It is simply asking too much to expect your assistant to know these things and to do a creditable job for you, without detailed knowledge of the case and explicit instructions as to how to proceed.

Some attorneys even compound the error by telling their assistant: "In addition, you decide what documents we need and see if you can get the other side to admit some of the facts we know are so. I'll take the depositions—after you decide who is to be deposed—but you get everything else ready."

The assistant will leave the room with head whirling and in a state of bewilderment. He or she will seek help from the first kind person he or she meets who will explain just what has to be done. Both of them may hope that in their ignorance of what you have in mind they are doing the right thing.

This sounds like an extravagant example, but is it? Haven't you done this from time to time—and don't you have an acquaintance who does it all the time? It could be called the Big Shot Syndrome. To test yourself, just ask your secretary if you have ever done anything like this to him or her. You may be surprised to observe how quickly he or she answers "yes."

This is no way to work with your associate. You must limit your demands to one subject—i.e., interrogatories, or a motion to produce—and then you must narrow your instructions even more by limiting the scope of the immediate task to one aspect of the subject matter. If you are dealing with the production of documents, tell your assistant to get those documents you need from one opponent before you turn your attention to another one, or within one time period, or one class of documents, leaving to a later date your instructions pertaining to another class. I'm talking here about your instructions to your assistant, not about filing pleadings in court. The actual work-product can be as lengthy, complicated and all-inclusive as you desire, but in the preparatory stage—for goodness' sake and your assistant's sake—break it into manageable and understandable portions.

TAKE TIME TO COMMUNICATE

As you can appreciate, all these things require communication. You have to talk to make yourself heard. You have to meet so that you can talk. At these meetings you have to explain what you want, answer questions, give directions regarding the best way to get the information you want, analyze the work that has been done to date, and criticize.

Certainly this takes time. No one ever said that your having an assistant means that you don't have to work on a file at all! It only means that now you don't have to spend a great deal of time on the detail work on one case, but instead can supervise the work on several cases at once. But, to supervise, you have to communicate. Accordingly, plan on a regular schedule of meetings. You could arrange to get together after your assistant has completed a particular assignment, or you could meet daily or biweekly at a specified time. However you care to do it is a matter of personal choice—just do it! Your assistant cannot read your mind, and you will never know whether the work is proceeding well or poorly unless the two of you get together and talk about it. That is your opportunity to make corrections in whatever work is being done, to give additional facts to your assistant, and to give new directions, if necessary, to the course of the work.

However you care to do it, good communication between you and your paralegal is essential.

REVIEW THE CASE IN DETAIL

The first important step in working with your paralegal is to go over the case in detail. If your assistant doesn't understand what the case is all about, he or she cannot do any assigned task really well. With regard to your explanation of the facts of the case, a word of warning is appropriate right now: do not give your assistant the file with instructions to read it, and with the expectation that once having done so he or she will know all about the case. That is not true and you know it is not true. If you are the one who took in the case, met with the client and, possibly, a member of the family or a friendly witness, you know very well that fully one-quarter to one-third of the information about the case is in your head and not in the file. This is where the need for communication is vital. I remember very clearly several incidents of this kind when, as a young attorney, I was working with a senior partner of the law firm. When we were discussing my handling of a case of his I might mention an essential fact that was missing in our case, to which he would respond: "Oh, we have that," or, "Didn't I mention that?" The answer was, "No, you didn't mention that," and it was frustrating in the extreme. (In retrospect I hope I barked out that answer, or said it caustically; but as I recall, the words were spoken definitely but with a degree of discretion and deference. Perhaps you know what I mean.) In either event the facts that I didn't know completely fouled up the work I had done. It was as simple as that. So, certainly, let your assistant begin with a reading of the file since it contains all the basic information, but follow that up with a meeting at which you can explain the several matters that are not in the file but in your head.

At the conclusion of that meeting your assistant should have all the information that is known, at that time, about the case. You should also have expressed some cautions about those aspects of it on which you have doubts, and should discuss the extent of your client's knowledge and its likely accuracy and completeness. Talking about the client in this way gives your assistant a "feel" or a "sense" for the person and enables him or her to develop an intuition about the case. I do believe in intuition but not as a novel, somewhat weird kind of extra-sensory perception. I perceive it as a judgmental reaction based on one's knowledge and experience. Intuition, so defined, is a valuable aid in making decisions, and its formation begins at this time, when you and your assistant go over every fact, evaluate the client, and engage in conversation about what might have occurred and how you are going to find out what, in fact, did occur.

HAVE YOUR ASSISTANT PREPARE A LIST OF KNOWN AND PROVABLE FACTS

If you are lost in the woods someday, a good way to get back to civilization is to take the time to try to figure out where you are. You can study a map, take compass readings, look for prominent terrain features, watch the movement of the sun, or whatever. But first figure out where you are rather than aimlessly wandering about just hoping that, by luck, you will find your way.

So with the start of a new case. Before you invoke discovery have your paralegal prepare a list of all known—and provable—facts. At this stage it doesn't do any good to list a fact that you are pretty sure is true, but can't prove. The Request for Admissions exists as a discovery tool for just such a purpose. For now, just stay with the facts you can prove. Preparing such a list is an excellent way for your helper to organize his or her thoughts and, seeing them in black and white, to begin to think about all the facts he or she cannot prove and how to go about securing those facts. It's a good way to begin to plan your work.

Let us take a simple automobile intersection accident for illustration. Your assistant might prepare a list like this:

KNOWN AND PROVABLE FACTS

1. Accident occurred on September 6, 198—, at 2:00 P.M.
2. Intersection of Elm and First Avenue.
3. Plaintiff proceeding East on Elm Street.
4. Defendant proceeding North on First Avenue.
5. A stop sign exists on Elm Street at the intersection.
6. Plaintiff driving a 1980 Buick Sedan.
7. Defendant driving a dark Cadillac.
8. Weather conditions: sunny, clear, dry.
9. James Jones saw the accident and assisted Plaintiff.
10. Plaintiff's car badly damaged at right front—fender, hood and wheel.
11. No passengers in Plaintiff's car.
12. Plaintiff was into the intersection when the collision occurred.
13. Plaintiff was badly injured; could not get out of car; ambulance arrived and crew removed him from car.

Suppose for a moment that these are all the facts that you can prove at this time. It takes only a moment to realize that there are a host of things you don't know. Where in the intersection did the accident occur? Was there a traffic control signal for cars traveling on First Avenue? What did the witness, James Jones, observe? Were there any other witnesses? How fast were the respective vehicles going? Where were the Plaintiff and Defendant coming from and going to? Was either of them in a hurry? What was the point of impact on Defendant's car?

One would go on with a dozen more similar questions. They all need to be answered. The important point is that by making out a list such as the one above, your assistant can recognize how many facts are not known.

Let us take one moment for an aside about a comparison of the state of the attorney's general knowledge with that of his paralegal assistant. Just by glancing at the facts of this elemental, basic—one might almost say "grade school"—legal problem the mind of the attorney recognizes the issues, the facts he needs, and the discovery techniques he will use to get the facts. Almost without thinking he knows that he must prepare interrogatories to get the identity of witnesses and other data known to defendant, order a police report, file a Motion to Produce to get the itemized repair bill for defendant's car, take a deposition of defendant and send an investigator out to interview Mr. Jones and the crew of the ambulance.

Unfortunately, the average paralegal, who does not have a considerable amount of experience, doesn't think along these lines with the rapidity and understanding of the lawyer. This is why consultation with the lawyer and instructions from him are so important.

Returning to the illustrative problem, you can see that by listing the known, provable facts the paralegal can begin to understand how many additional details will be needed.

As one examines the complexity of a case one realizes how much more difficult things become for the paralegal and how necessary it is to divide the proposed work into understandable portions that can be effectively handled, and to give direction as to how one wants the information collected—i.e., the discovery process to be utilized.

EXPLAIN THE APPLICABLE LAW

When your assistant has a clear understanding of the facts of the case, it is necessary to explain the general principles of law applicable to those facts. Without such an explanation your paralegal will fail to understand the context in which the facts are going to be used and why some are more important than others. Thus, in our hypothetical intersection case, you could explain the duties of each driver as he came to the intersection and why it is important to learn which of them was committed to the intersection first; you might point out the requirements of statutes regulating speeds as they apply if this intersection is in a school zone, a residential area, or along a major highway. It might be helpful to discuss the use of a police report as evidence, and, if a Business Records Act or local rule prescribes certain formalities for using it, how one can comply with those requirements. In addition, if either party made an admission at the scene of the accident, you could point out how important that could be as evidence of liability.

With a little knowledge of this kind the whole process of discovery becomes more sensible to your assistant. Now he or she is not merely trying to ascertain a fact, but is collecting a fact that has a certain meaning to the overall case. In other words, the work begins to make sense.

A discussion of this kind can also help your assistant to know that certain information is positively essential (did plaintiff stop at the "stop sign?); other matters are interesting and informative but not really vital (had plaintiff received medical treatment in the past to any parts of his anatomy injured in this accident?); and some data is for general background only (date of birth, place of employment, Social Security number).

It is good for all of us to bear in mind that facts in and of themselves do not have much significance. After a little understanding of the applicable law, however, the facts become important and it becomes clear that they have differing degrees of importance.

DISCUSS YOUR THEORY OF LIABILITY OR DEFENSE

At the beginning of every case, I'm sure that you can think of several different theories by which the case might be won. Naturally the key to success is in developing sufficient evidence to justify your proceeding to trial on one theory rather than another. While your paralegal is helping you to gather the evidence, he or she ought to know what approach you are taking. This is another area in which misapprehension can lead to wasted time and energy. Therefore, it behooves you to explain just how you intend to win this case and the facts that you need to accomplish that purpose. Referring once again to our hypothetical example, a Plaintiff's attorney might say:

> Look, we'll work on the idea that defendant was traveling at a high rate of speed; that he saw Plaintiff stop and then proceed into the intersection; that he thought Plaintiff would clear the intersection in time and when he didn't our defendant could not stop and the accident occurred.

That is a good theory. Your assistant, after additional instructions, can now begin to utilize the appropriate discovery methods to support this hypothesis. Now suppose you also order some investigation and the investigator learns from witness Jones that the defendant was proceeding at a very sensible speed, that it appeared to Jones that defendant tried to apply his brakes to slow down for the intersection, that the brakes didn't work and thus the collision. Jones even tried to operate the brakes of defendant's car after the accident, while moving it to the curb, and the brakes were inoperable.

At this point your original theory is no longer valid, and you're going to have to switch to a new one involving the brakes on defendant's car. You might even start wondering whether defendant's brakes were improperly repaired recently, and consider the possibility of your bringing a mechanic or repair garage into the case.

Immediately you will have to call in your paralegal, explain the newly received information, stop the work on the earlier theory, and start all over again with a new hypothesis of liability and a whole new approach to the discovery necessary to support this concept.

The point is that you have to keep your assistant apprised of changes in the case, of new and different ideas you have, and of what you want him or her to do now. Don't keep the poor soul in the dark and then get upset when you are presented with a nice set of discovery documents that have nothing whatsoever to do with your current ideas.

The same sort of thing can happen to you as a defense attorney. You start off with the idea that Plaintiff failed to stop before entering the intersection and put your paralegal to work on that theory. Then you discover that he did stop, but started again like the proverbial jack-rabbit and shot in front of your defendant. You had better call in your assistant and explain the change in circumstances and in approach.

Whatever the case may be, and irrespective of your position as representing either a plaintiff or a defendant, you have to have a theory of liability or defense and your assistant has to be thoroughly conversant with it. When it changes due to changing circumstances, don't keep that a secret. Let your paralegal know about the change so that there isn't a waste of time and effort.

OUTLINE THE FACTS NEEDED TO SUPPORT YOUR THEORY

Once you have decided where you are going, the next step is to figure out how to get there; having determined upon a theory of liability or defense you are now faced with the task of accumulating the facts you need to support it. This involves a little more than determining the facts you need, comparing this list with the facts you have, and then itemizing the ones you still need. The question is: how do you get them?

The easiest way to handle this is to prepare an outline that will sketch out what you need and how you propose to get it. This accomplishes two purposes—it clarifies your thinking and represents a work schedule for your assistant, and, equally important, it almost automatically breaks down the work into definable, easily understood objectives for your assistant.

The outline need not be lengthy, but it should be complete. For example, turning again to our automobile case, you could work up something like this:

FACTS NEEDED
1. Speed of defendant as he approached intersection.
2. Speed of defendant immediately prior to accident.
3. Condition of brakes after accident.

4. If they are defective:
    a) Did the accident damage them?
    b) Was the defect a pre-existent condition?
    c) Should the defendant have known of their condition?
    d) Was it a sudden emergency situation?
5. Words or conduct of defendant at the scene.
6. Repairs to brakes—who, when, why and nature of repairs.
7. Witnesses.
8. Areas of damage to defendant's car and cost of repair.
9. Background information regarding defendant.
10. Any evidence of drinking or drunkedness.
11. Where defendant was coming from and going to.
12. General data regarding car—age, condition, mileage.
13. Data regarding the scene of the accident.

You should prepare a list like this with your assistant so that there is a clear understanding between you concerning what you are looking for.

EXPLORE TOGETHER THE BEST WAYS TO GET THE INFORMATION YOU NEED

After you have your outline prepared, the next topic for discussion is how you are going to get the information. This is the time when the attorney has to begin giving instructions. It will be easy for him to select the most appropriate discovery tool for each type of fact. Look over that list of facts needed. It would appear that No. 3, "Condition of brakes after accident," No. 4, "If they are defective..," No. 5, "Words or conduct of defendant at the scene," and No. 13, "Data regarding the scene of the accident" can best be secured by investigation and supplemented by the deposition of the defendant. A deposition should also be used to secure Nos. 1 and 2, "Speed of defendant as he approached the intersection and immediately prior to the accident," No. 6, "Repairs to brakes..," and No. 11, "Where defendant was coming from and going to." Interrogatories can be used for No. 7, "Witnesses," No. 9, "Background information regarding defendant," and No. 12, "General data regarding car.." You will probably file a Motion to Produce a repair bill or estimate to secure the answer to No. 8, "Areas of damage to defendant's car.." and possibly No. 6, "Repairs to brakes...."

You can then give your assistant a simple outline that will determine not only the facts that he or she must collect but also the way to do it. The work is laid out for the paralegal. Something like this will do fine:

Interrogatories—Nos. 7, 9 and 12
Investigation—Nos. 3, 4, 5 and 13
Deposition—Nos. 1, 2, 3, 4, 5, 6 and 11
Motion to produce—Nos. 6 and 8

Your assistant can now leave you alone and begin to work with a clear idea of what he or she is doing. In due course of time the discovery will be underway with a reasonable likelihood that it will be effective and productive.

Don't forget that there is a certain element of priority to these discovery techniques. Thus investigation and interrogatories are generally used first, followed by the deposition. A motion to produce can only be filed after you learn what data is available and who has it. This is probably going to be after you have taken the deposition or received the answers to interrogatories. Last of all will be your Requests for Admissions; these will be filed to establish a fact already known or strongly suspected and thus avoid proof at trial, rather than to seek after facts.

STUDY THE RESULTS, ANALYZE THEM, REGROUP AND MOVE AHEAD

When opposing counsel begins to answer the interrogatories, when the investigation report comes in, and when documents are produced for inspection, it is time again to meet with your assistant to analyze this information. What have you learned and where do you stand now? It is to be expected that you will be disappointed with some of the information you received, while other data will be very helpful. It is time to talk over different ideas. Perhaps your theory of liability or defense will change again; possibly you will have discovered another party who ought to be brought into the case; and inevitably you will come up with new questions you want answered, another deposition to be taken, or documents secured from some other person or organization. It is from such a meeting that you outline the additional data you want and determine how your paralegal will secure it.

It is also a time to criticize—objectively, dispassionately and in a friendly manner. You may well observe that the interrogatories were too vague and imprecise; that the motion to produce was so broad that it evoked a motion for a protective order that you will now have to argue; or, just as bad, that you now have a stack of documents on your desk which you have to go through, well knowing that most of them are not of help.

This is your opportunity to sharpen the skills of your assistant by pointing out the errors and correcting them. It does no good to keep still if mistakes have been made, but at the same time incentive is destroyed by harsh criticism.

At any rate, after you have made a thorough review of the new information and adjusted your plans, it's time to get back to the next step in the discovery process.

DISCOVERY IS A CONTINUING PROCESS UNTIL YOU HAVE ALL THE DATA YOU NEED—OR CAN GET

Fortunately there are no rules that allow you only a single chance at any given discovery technique. The answers to interrogatories will lead to your additional questions and to a motion to produce. The documents produced will compel you to take a deposition, and this in turn may lead you to order more investigation. It's an on-going process and it ends only when you have all the information you need. Thus, it's important that you keep in close contact with your assistant—prodding, advising, correcting, supervising. Your paralegal will do the work if, between the two of you, there is a clear understanding of what's to be done and how it fits into the overall case. While the role of the assistant is to do the work, the job of the attorney is to guide and direct. Together you can have the pleasure of a case successfully concluded and a satisfied client. In addition, if you have worked well as a team you will have furthered a relationship that will continue to lead to happy results in the future.

Chapter 3

Building a Solid Foundation—the Imaginative Use of Interrogatories

The Trial Lawyer should always keep in mind the following facts:

INTERROGATORIES ARE THE FOUNDATION BLOCKS
OF SUCCESSFUL CASES.

★ ★ ★ ★ ★

THEY ARE A POTENT AND EFFECTIVE TOOL.

★ ★ ★ ★ ★

THEY ARE FREE OF CHARGE.

★ ★ ★ ★ ★

If there were ever three good reasons for putting time and effort into a project that can only benefit you, these three should be persuasive. Yet, for some reason, many attorneys refuse to work at preparing a good set of Interrogatories.

Let me emphasize that Interrogatories are to Discovery as foundation blocks are to a house—unglamorous but necessary; they provide the support for the whole structure. In addition, like foundation stones in construction they come first. There is a good reason for this: one has to have some general background information and some basic data before one can engage in probing, carefully thought out, and case-winning depositions. Interrogatories are the foot soldiers of discovery, setting up the opponent for the sudden, decisive cavalry charge; in football parlance they are the running backs who continually pound away for a few yards until the linebackers and defensive backs begin to move up, thus setting the scene for the long touchdown pass.

Interrogatories are important, detailed, and somewhat laborious to prepare. As in all such office work they are often glossed over, done hurriedly, and viewed with some distaste—one might almost say active dislike—by many lawyers. What a mistake!

FORCE YOUR OPPONENT TO WORK FOR YOU—FOR FREE!

It is often said that nothing is free in this world. That's not true. The Answers to Interrogatories are free. Think of this for a moment: where else in the law (or in the world for that matter) can you force your opponent to work for you—with no payment expected or required! It happens every time you serve a set of Interrogatories. It is perfectly proper for you to prepare a set of Interrogatories that could have your opposition pulling his hair and shouting imprecations, but at the same time tearing apart records, interviewing people, holding meetings, and, in short, working for you to secure those mandatory answers to your questions. You can have fun with this discovery tool if you want to. But seriously, you are literally forcing the defendant (or plaintiff) to gather information that you need to win your lawsuit. He may not like it, but he has to do it.

HOW INTERROGATORIES CAN HELP YOU TO WIN YOUR CASE

Certainly the primary function of Interrogatories is to gather information—the necessary facts that your opponent knows and you do not. At the same time, however, you should always ask some very probing questions that touch on the most sensitive aspects of your liability problem and thus, hopefully, secure an answer that will win your case right then and there! Many attorneys are shy about this for some reason that has never been clear to me. Unless you ask a searching question there will never be an opportunity for the other side to come forward with the answer. This is clearly one instance in which the Biblical admonition still applies: *Ask and you shall receive.* You can rely on the fact that in most instances your opponent will respond to your question truthfully and accurately, so if you do ask a question that goes to the heart of the matter you may well get an admission that will end the case. Settlements result when your opponent is forced to admit that he is liable, or, if you represent a defendant, that your client is not liable in the cause of action that is the subject matter of the lawsuit. When you receive an answer that is obviously damaging to the cause of your adversary, the subject matter of negotiation quickly switches from "Are we liable?" to "How much (or little) shall we pay?" Let us consider some actual instances in which specific Interrogatories resulted in cases being won very quickly.

ILLUSTRATION NO. 1—A Student Rider Thrown from a Horse

The plaintiff went to a prestigious riding academy to take horseback riding lessons. She stated that she was taking a lesson at the indoor ring under the supervision of the instructor when the horse suddenly veered or jerked to the right, throwing the rider to the ground and resulting in her injuring a cervical disc. She stated that there was no apparent reason for the horse to have made the sudden movement. She also mentioned that hers was the first lesson of the day at the academy.

The plaintiff's attorney discussed the incident with an experienced instructor, who advised him to make inquiry in four areas:

1. Was the horse kept in a box stall or a standup stall? The significance here is that the horse can lie down and rest in a box stall, which can contribute to its being a more tranquil and contented animal.

2. Was the horse exercised prior to the beginning of the lessons? This is important because a horse tends to be nervous and skittish in the morning; horses suffer from the "early morning blahs" just as people do.

3. Did the instructor use a lunge line? A lunge line is a rope, 30 feet or so in length, whereby the instructor maintains some control over the horse.

4. Did the horse have a bad reputation for throwing students or other riders?

Please note two things about these questions: first, an expert was consulted, who suggested the areas into which inquiry should be directed; and second, the questions would have to be tailored to the specific facts of the case. There are no "Form Interrogatories" that can be designed to apply to an accident of this kind. Certainly the average attorney is not going to have enough cases of this kind to justify the preparation of Form Interrogatories. The Interrogatories that were submitted included the following:

1. Identify the horse here involved, including the following:
   a) The name of the horse;
   b) Date of birth of the horse;
   c) Identity of the farm or stable at which it was reared;
   d) The date of purchase of this horse by the Defendant (if it was purchased);
   e) The uses to which the horse has been put by the Defendant during the time it has owned the horse.

ANSWER:

    a) Snoopy.

    b) November 10, 1976.

    c) Sunny Slopes Farm.

    d) December 1, 1980.

    e) Used for riding by students and other members of the public.

2. State whether the horse here involved was, on the night before this accident, kept in a box stall or a standup stall.

ANSWER:

This horse was kept in a box stall.

3. State whether the riding lesson scheduled for Mrs. Jones was the first riding lesson given at the Defendant's academy on the day of the accident.

ANSWER:

Yes.

4. Set forth the time at which Plaintiff's riding lesson began.

ANSWER:

8:00 A.M.

5. State whether prior to the time the riding lesson began the horse here involved was exercised, and if the answer is "yes," set forth:

    a) The identity of the person who exercised the horse.

    b) The time at which the horse was exercised.

    c) The length of time during which the horse was exercised.

ANSWER:

    a) John Riley, stable hand.

    b) Approximately between 6:30 A.M. and 8:00 A.M. Exact time unknown.

    c) Approximately 30 minutes.

6. Identify the name and home address of the person who was instructing the Plaintiff at the time of this accident.

ANSWER:

Mary Brown
123 White Street
Pittsburgh, Pennsylvania.

7. State whether the instructor utilized a lunge line during the period of instruction.

ANSWER:

No.

8. State whether the Defendant has any knowledge of any student or rider being thrown from or falling from the horse here involved

prior to the date of this accident, and if the answer is "yes," set forth:

a) The name and home address of persons who have been thrown from or who have fallen from this horse.

b) The date of each such incident.

c) Whether the rider was injured.

d) Whether any claim has been made against the Defendant by such rider.

ANSWER: Yes.

a) John Smith
456 Jones Street
Aspinwall, Pennsylvania.

Susan Black
789 Oriole Drive
Pittsburgh, Pennsylvania.

Joan Calgani
10 Somerset Blvd.
Pleasant Hills, Pennsylvania.

b) John Smith-April 14, 1981.
Susan Black-January 23, 1981.
Joan Calgani-December 20, 1980

c) John Smith-Injured.
Susan Black-Injured.
Joan Calgani-Injured.

d) John Smith and Susan Black have filed claims against this Defendant.

You will note from the answers that Plaintiff's counsel struck out regarding the questions about the box stall and the exercising of the horse, but the answers to the questions about the lunge line and prior accidents were pure gold. Since the instructor did not use a lunge line she had no control whatsoever over the movements of the horse, and we now know that the horse had thrown three other riders. Clearly the academy had prior notice that this horse was trouble.

The answers to those two questions provided all the ammunition Plaintiff's counsel needed on liability. As a result, this case was settled promptly and for a substantial sum.

It is important to note that in this case proper specific questions were asked. The defendant could have avoided, evaded or even lied in its answers—but it did not. You will find that in 99 percent of the cases the defendant will not do so. The answers were straightforward and liability attached.

ILLUSTRATION NO. 2—An Electrical Arc Case

In this case the plaintiff was a painter whose duty it was to paint a tower carrying high voltage electrical lines, at a substation owned by a major public utility. Aside from the usual warning sign attached to the fence surrounding the tower, there were no other particular instructions given him. He related that about twenty feet up the tower there was a crossarm, on the outer edges of which electric wires were strung. The wires were attached by a ceramic device that looked like an inverted cup. The painter clung to a vertical beam and painted one side of it and then he began to move out on the horizontal beam, planning to paint it from its outer edge back toward the vertical beam. He took a few steps and was about four or five feet from the outer edge of the horizontal beam when he was struck by a bolt of electricity, thrown to the ground, and sustained injuries. He swore that he never touched the wires or the ceramic object. The facts seemed unusual—even weird. Can electricity jump and literally chase a man along a tower?

Inquiry to electrical engineers revealed that the device at the end of the horizontal beam is known as a "pothead," and that electricity can indeed arc over a distance of several feet and strike a person. They suggested that questions be asked of the defendant concerning why the electricity was not shut off at the tower; why the painters were not warned of the danger of arcing; and why barricades of some kind were not erected to keep the painters away from the "potheads" while they worked.

As a result of these conversations, some specific questions were prepared:

1. State whether the electrical power was shut off on the tower here involved while it was being painted.

ANSWER:

No.

2. State whether the device which holds the electric wires to the tower is known as a "pothead."

ANSWER:

Yes.

3. Set forth the amount of the voltage in the electric lines passing over the tower here involved at the time of this accident.

ANSWER:

25,000 volts.

4. State whether defendant knows that an electrical arc can be formed between the "pothead" and a person five feet away.

ANSWER:

Yes.

5. Set forth whether any person to the defendant's knowledge gave instructions to the plaintiff with regard to the risks, hazards or dangers of working near or around "potheads."

ANSWER:

Not to the knowledge of this Defendant.

6. Set forth whether there were any signs on or around the tower here involved warning persons concerning the danger of getting near the "potheads."

ANSWER:

A sign posted on the fence surrounding the tower reads:

"High Voltage—Keep Away."

7. State whether there were any barricades or restraining devices of any kind to keep the painters from getting close to the "potheads."

ANSWER:

None.

8. If there were signs or other written notice of hazards placed on or around the tower here involved, please set forth:

a) The exact wording on the signs;
b) The precise location of each and every sign.

ANSWER:

See answer to Number 6 above.

9. On the tower here involved and at the point where this accident happened, state whether there were any physical barriers, either wooden, rope or otherwise, to prevent plaintiff from stepping beyond the vertical beams of the tower.

ANSWER:

None.

As you can see, when the Defendant admitted that it knew that an arc could jump between the pothead and the place at which the Plaintiff was standing and that it neither warned Plaintiff of this nor shut down the electricity nor roped off the area near the potheads, the game was over. Realistically, where was the defense? Here again, because of a good set of Interrogatories the case was settled.

Consider for a moment that if the Interrogatories had not been asked, each of the cases set forth above could have dragged on for many months, possibly to the time of trial, before the facts became known and settlement became a practical reality. As it was, very early in the case this discovery tool was used and promptly after the answers were received a settlement was achieved.

ILLUSTRATION NO. 3—A Defective Intravenous Catheter

A catheter is nothing more than a tube designed to carry fluids. Its insertion into the human body is sometimes difficult, and manufacturers have developed various products to accomplish this purpose as easily as possible. In this case an injured woman had a catheter inserted into a vein in the area of the right collar bone—a subclavian jugular catheter. Unfortunately the catheter broke and moved, and the doctors had a very difficult time removing it at surgery. Since the attending physician insisted that he had inserted the catheter properly, the question arose whether the product was defective. Among the Interrogatories asked were these:

1. Has this Defendant received any complaints concerning its catheter, Model No. 1234?

ANSWER:

Yes.

2. If the answer to the foregoing question is "yes," set forth:

    a) The date of each and every complaint received by Defendant concerning this catheter;
    b) The name and address of the complaining party;
    c) The nature of the complaint.

ANSWER:

[the answer to this question consisted of a long list of persons who had made complaints to the company, most of which were substantially similar in nature to the complaint of the doctor in the instant case.]

3. Has this catheter ever been recalled by the Defendant either voluntarily or at the request of any governmental agency?

ANSWER:

Yes, voluntarily.

4. If the answer to the question above is "yes," set forth:

    a) The date of the recall;
    b) The reason for the recall.

ANSWER:

    a) June 26, 1980
    b) Sometime in 1980, Jones Manufacturing Co. began to receive complaints through a product complaint reporting service initiated by the Food & Drug Administration and the U.S. Pharmacopeia and also complaints directly from hospitals of problems relating to the adapter end of the catheter. An analysis of these

complaints indicated that they were generally caused by errors of the physicians who were using the catheter. These errors consisted either of the insertion of the wrong end of the catheter through the needle and into the patient or of insufficient tightening of the adapter end of the catheter to the adapter. As a result of this, a "product recall" was initiated by Jones Manufacturing Co., which amounted to a change in the directions for use of the catheter to explicitly point out that the metal end of the catheter must be attached to the screw-on adapter and that the catheter must be snugly applied, even if this required the use of a hemostat.

As you can imagine, the doctor was exonerated in this case and a quick settlement was effected with the manufacturer. The complaints of the other doctors and the problems they had were nearly the same as the difficulties experienced in the instant case so that there was plenty of notice to the manufacturer. Then, to top it off, the recall date was just a few weeks before this unfortunate plaintiff had the catheter inserted into her upper chest.

These three illustrations—just a few among many that could be selected—illustrate that your cases can be won through the use of interrogatories and at a very early stage in its life as a lawsuit.

The important point to be made is that you don't have to hold onto a case clear up to the time of trial, which in some states is many months—or even years—after the date of filing. In most instances you can have a good set of interrogatories prepared within 30 days after the Complaint is filed. Then if we allow another 30 days for your opponent to answer and a month or so for settlement negotiations, it is very possible to conclude a case in 90 days, give or take a few.

There is absolutely no good reason for many cases to linger for years. The lawyer is earning no money, or very little, while the case sits; the client is unhappy with the delay; and the court has one more case overloading its dockets. All that it takes to clear away this unfortunate and unnecessary state of affairs is for the lawyer—you—to prepare a detailed, specific set of questions, which your opponent must answer at no cost to you—and many of these cases can be brought to a prompt conclusion. If you are a defense attorney you can move for a Summary Judgment or Judgment on the Pleadings based on the answers to interrogatories. The principal value of the questions—and the answers—is that they force both parties to look at the strengths and weaknesses of their respective cases, and this encourages settlement. Many times your opposing counsel will not have really thought out his case or considered its problems until he or she has to make serious inquiries, ask tough questions, or search for documents to answer the questions. Just consider the position of the defense attorney in the case involving the lady who was thrown from the horse, when he had to ask his client about prior, similar incidents and learned that there were three such incidents, two of which involved claims against the riding academy. You know that very promptly he did three things: he opened settlement discussions with plaintiff's counsel, he notified his insurance carrier about the problem, and he told the client to get rid of the horse! Had the interrogatories not been served, it is very likely that none of those things would have been done and the case would have dragged on and on.

So interrogatories can accomplish a great deal for you. Frequently the answers will lead to settlement, but even if they do not they will certainly give you valuable information that you do need in the preparation of your case for trial.

THERE ARE SEVERAL ADVANTAGES TO USING INTERROGATORIES INSTEAD OF INVESTIGATION

Interrogatories can never replace investigation but they can reduce the amount of investigation that you require. Let's face it—private investigators are expensive and their cost is going up, not down. To the extent that you can use Interrogatories to do your investigation, your costs will be reduced. Obviously that is an important consideration. There is one other aspect of this question of Interrogatory vs. Investigation that you might think about: when you send out an investigator he asks the questions his way; when you prepare Interrogatories you are asking the questions the way you want them asked. The difference can be very significant in terms of the answer you are looking for.

Finally, we must always keep in mind that your opposing party will be answering the Interrogatories and he, she, or it is going to be bound by those answers. The question and answer can be read into evidence during the trial. That is not true of an investigation report. Usually your investigator does not take sworn statements from the people he talks with; such persons can change their minds or claim to have been misquoted, and you're not going to read the investigation report into evidence.

These represent a few more good reasons for the careful preparation of interrogatories.

USE INTERROGATORIES TO UNCOVER STATIC FACTS

Interrogatories have a limited capacity; they are useful to uncover fixed, unchangeable, what may be referred to as "static," facts. In the very nature of things you can't use them to engage in dialogue with your opponent; save that for depositions. If you try it sometime you will soon learn that you can go crazy trying to come up with alternative questions in anticipation of your opponent's answers. And you lay yourself open to sarcastic or comic answers, to wit:

Q: When you came to the intersection of First Avenue and Green Street, which way did you go?

A: Through the intersection.

Q: Why did you proceed in that direction?

A: To get to the other side!

That's not very helpful—but it's an honest answer.
Or this:

Q: Of the four recognized methods to perform this operation, which did you use?

A: Method No. 2.

Q: Why did you choose this technique?

A: To save the man's life.

What does one do with that answer?

It's no good. Your opponent can always answer a "why" question in a way that can evade, hurt or embarrass you. Don't give him or her the chance. Besides, such questions are a complete waste of time. They lead nowhere and provide no useful information.

Interrogatories are best used to answer the questions "who," "what," "when," and "where." Leave the "hows" and "whys" for depositions.

With these limitations, however, you are free to explore every facet of your lawsuit—to uncover information you don't have and to prove facts that you know are essential to your case.

YOU ARE NOT LIMITED TO INFORMATION THAT IS DIRECTLY RELATED TO THE ISSUES IN THE CASE

Don't be timid about asking questions and seeking information. You are not limited to questions that directly relate to the issues involved in the lawsuit. Remember that this is *discovery*—the purpose of which is to uncover all information you need. The rule is clear; you can discover information which, while not directly relevant, can lead to facts that are relevant to the lawsuit. This is very important; without this right your ability to gather information would be quite restricted and you might not learn some helpful information. Suppose you have a case in which the condition of the plaintiff's heart is very much at issue. It stands to reason that you can ask all sorts of questions about prior medical treatment of the plaintiff—examinations, diagnostic techniques, hospitalizations, drugs and medications and restrictions on activities. But can you ask such questions about the parents of plaintiff? His brothers and sisters? Absolutely. There is a respected body of medical opinion that believes that certain heart conditions are hereditary in nature and that therefore your questions inquiring into familial difficulties with cardiac conditions are perfectly proper.

The same thing applies to prior difficulties with an instrumentality. Suppose your client was injured in a large department store when an elevator malfunctioned. Certainly you want to know all about the elevator on the day of the accident—but it is equally proper to inquire about prior accidents or malfunctions both as to this elevator and as to other similar ones in the store. Suppose the store has four Otis elevators. Let us additionally assume that the Plaintiff was hurt on Otis No. 2 due to some supposed defect in the operating mechanism. You are certainly justified in asking all the questions you deem pertinent as to Otis No. 2. If you suspect that the same defect existed in the other Otis elevators and that the store had prior notice of the condition, you can interrogate as to the other Otis elevators—inspections, maintenance, repairs, accidents, complaints to Otis, and anything else you think can help you. All of these questions may *lead you* to information that will be relevant to your case—questions of Notice and the like—and these questions constitute permissible discovery.

REMEMBER!

1. Interrogatories should be the first discovery tool you use.
2. You force the opposition to work for you—free of charge.
3. Use interrogatories as an inexpensive substitute for investigation.
4. Use it to uncover static facts:
     Who
     What
     Where
     When
5. The opposing party is bound by the answers to interrogatories.
6. You have the opportunity to frame the questions in your own style.
7. You are not limited to facts directly related to the lawsuit but can inquire into matters that will lead to such facts.

AN ILLUSTRATION OF THE ABUSE OF DISCOVERY

We were discussing, a few moments ago, a theoretical accident in an Otis elevator located in a department store. If we may digress for a moment from a discussion of proper discovery we can use that example to demonstrate an abuse of discovery that is becoming quite prevelant. Suppose the department store contained additional elevators manufactured and installed by, let us say, Westinghouse Corporation. Now if you decide to interrogate as to the Westinghouse elevators in the same manner as you did concerning the Otis elevators, a serious, practical, ethical problem is created. Certainly you have no reason to believe that the Westinghouse elevators had anything to do with the accident in which you are involved, or that they are constructed the same way or are of the same design as the Otis elevators. (You can legitimately inquire if this is true if you have doubts in the matter.) Nonetheless if you ask the questions you may be able to convince some judge that maybe—just maybe—there are significant similarities that justify your probing. This puts the judge in an uncomfortable position; even though he really doesn't believe it, nonetheless he doesn't want to restrict discovery if you think it's important. He isn't close enough to the facts to draw fine distinctions, so, applying the liberal construction rule, he lets you proceed. You may well force the defendant to spend many man-hours searching through old and current records and interviewing its maintenance men—and all for naught. You know, opposing counsel knows, and the department store knows that even if a prior accident on, or defect in, the Westinghouse equipment is found, it isn't going to help you. This is the kind of thing that brings discovery into disrepute. There is a certain discipline required of lawyers to avoid this sort of thing.

All of the above-mentioned strictures can be ignored if we just change the facts a little bit.

Suppose that the accident occurred because of a defect in the power source to all the elevators, or a breakdown in some master control panel. That one little change could make a world of difference; now it might well be necessary and appropriate to make inquiry about stoppages, breakdowns and accidents involving all the elevators—both Otis and Westinghouse.

As you can see, much depends on the factual basis with which you are confronted. Conduct that is justified under one set of circumstances is completely improper under a different set of facts. Attorneys have fine minds and habitually make discriminating judgments, and it is appropriate that they do so in deciding just when discovery reaches the boundary of proper conduct and begins to step into the forbidden zone of behavior that may not be malicious but is deliberately miserable.

I have just learned that there are some significant changes contemplated in the Discovery sections of the Federal Rules of Civil Procedure. These rule changes are aimed at correcting abuses of Discovery and include giving the District Court Judges the authority:

1. to limit Discovery after consideration of the issues involved, the importance of the case, the amount of money involved and the value of the information sought in relation to the amount of work needed to secure it;

2. to impose money sanctions on an attorney and/or litigant who is responsible for evasive responses to Discovery, harassment in its use, or extensive Discovery that is deliberately disproportionate to the information needed.

In other words, if one deliberately abuses Discovery in the future, it may cost the attorney, if he or she is at fault, or the client, some hard-earned money. This should be a step in the right direction toward avoiding some of the evasiveness and excesses that we now must contend with.

FORM INTERROGATORIES—HELP OR HINDRANCE?

I am slightly cynical about human nature and happen to believe in the adage that the less one has to do the less one does. If you take the fact that preparing interrogatories is hard work to begin with and throw in the enticement of a set of forms lying around the office, I will wager, and give odds, that the average person will use the forms every time even if half the questions have nothing to do with the lawsuit. I know this to be so. In Assumpsit cases I've received form interrogatories that asked questions about "prior medical treatment to the same part of the body involved herein," and in a trespass case involving a baby I've seen extensive questions about employment, wages, marital status, dependents and taxpayer's ID number. Let's fact it—forms are a lazy man's way of doing things. We start off with the best of intentions: let's draw up a set of basic questions for different kinds of cases and then for each specific case we will simply add the precise, pertinent questions relevant to that case. It sounds good, but it never works out as well as it sounds.

I believe that Interrogatories have to be expressly designed for the individual case—from scratch—and that you are only deceiving yourself if you think you can prepare forms that will do a creditable job in every case or, more importantly, that you will seriously and diligently add specific, searching questions to your forms.

The only justifiable exception to this rule is the large, high-volume law office that lives by forms or drowns in a sea of pleadings. This type of operation has to have forms, but the very reason for the need—a lack of time to give individual attention to each case—implies that even if specific questions are supposed to be added they probably won't be, or only a few will be tacked on in a slap-dash manner. As an individual attorney you should enjoy seeing form interrogatories come to your office from opposing counsel; it is a clear signal that the lawyer is too busy to pay significant attention to this one case and that he or she is susceptible to some important blunders. It's just a little matter to keep in mind.

I suspect that plaintiffs' attorneys are a little more inhibited in designing forms than are the defense attorneys. This is mainly because a plaintiff's lawyer is searching for facts regarding liability (which doesn't easily fit into categories) while a defense attorney is after facts pertaining to both liability and damages, and the latter can be categorized. Injuries and losses are relatively fixed items and therefore fit easily within the orbit of form interrogatories.

Despite my admonition some readers are going to opt for forms. So be it. If you are going to use them, let's decide what they should contain and then look at some sample forms, although the actual preparation of forms has to be a do-it-yourself project tailored to your specific needs and desires. Their scope and content will depend on the type of case you habitually handle (i.e., medical malpractice, automobile cases, sales of goods and merchandise, entertainment contracts); your personal attitude (do you want a lot of details or not?); and your goals (are you inquisitive about general background information or do you want to zero right in on the significant, vital issues?).

Another problem is that we tend to categorize our cases—Trespass and Assumpsit—according to "liability" or "type of incident" standards. Thus we speak of a "gas explosion" case, "medical malpractice," and an "intersection collision" in the field of personal injury law. The same is true of contract law: we refer to a financial transaction or a case involving defective goods or a breach of service contract. These terms identify the case in terms of "what happened," and that relates directly to questions involving liability.

As you can imagine, a plaintiff's attorney is very much restricted in preparing a form that will apply to all or several of these different causes of action; there just isn't much similarity between an airplane accident and a medical malpractice case. The only thing he can do is to analyze his volume of each type of case, and if the numbers indicate that there is a steady repetition of a particular class of cases, then he can prepare a set of form interrogatories for that style of action.

The defense attorney is in a little different situation; in every personal injury case a plaintiff has been injured, has received medical treatment, incurred bills for same, lost wages and, frequently, suffered a disability. This is true whether the loss occurred due to the collapse of the landing gear on an airplane or the slip of a surgeon's knife. Thus defense counsel can prepare a good set of form interrogatories encompassing matters of injury and loss to the plaintiff. On the liability side, however, he is in no better position than the plaintiff's attorney.

Since there are such a variety of types of lawsuits, let us try to categorize the information in terms of some other standard—need, perhaps. Thus in every trespass case—no matter what it is—we want to know about *Witnesses* and *Investigation* and *Documents*. A set of standard interrogatories for use in every such case for both plaintiff and defense counsel could be these:

I. Witnesses:

1. Identify by name and address each and every person known to the (opposing party) who witnessed the accident (incident) involved in this lawsuit.
2. Identify by name and address every person known to the (opposing party) who was a witness to events immediately preceding the accident (incident) involved in this lawsuit.
3. Identify by name and address every person known to the (opposing party) who was a witness to events immediately subsequent to the accident (incident) involved in this lawsuit.

This will serve to identify the witnesses—those who were at the scene when the accident occurred, the ones who came running up after the event, and those who just happened to be in the area beforehand.

Now let's get some information about the witnesses:

4. As to each person named in answer to interrogatories 1–3, identify those who were either a friend or relative to the (opposing party).
5. As to each witness named in answer to interrogatories 1–3, identify those persons from whom a written, or tape-recorded, statement has been taken by any person or organization to the knowledge of (opposing party) or on his behalf by his counsel, insurance carrier, investigators, family or friends.

6. As to each person identified in answer to Interrogatory No. 5, set forth:

   a. The date the statement was taken;
   b. The name and address of the person taking the statement;
   c. Whether the statement is in writing or was tape-recorded.
   d. The name and address of the person who presently has possession of the statement or tape;

> e. Whether the witness was paid any money, for whatever purpose, in connection with, or relating to, the giving of the statement.

These last two questions—Interrogatories No. 5 and No. 6—raise a question about you and your relations with the other members of your Bar and the style of practice in your community. Is it relaxed and friendly or hostile and hypertechnical? The difference could affect the way one phrases these questions—and others like them. The questions refer to a "written statement" or "tape recording."

There are other ways to collect information. An investigator could prepare a summary of his conversation with a witness—that's not necessarily a written statement; a telephone call could be made to a witness and notes made of the conversation or a stenographic transcript made of the conversation—that's not a tape recording. In my jurisdiction the Plaintiff's Bar and Defense Bar are composed of excellent lawyers who dispute mightily over the issues but who do not bother with minutae or split hairs in matters involving discovery. I know that the questions, as framed, would draw forth from opposing counsel an answer that would include whatever information he had, however secured. He knows what the questions are driving at and he is willing to produce the data. That may not be true in your jurisdiction. In certain areas hypertechnicality, hair-splitting and nit-picking are a way of life. That's unfortunate. If you must practice in such an area then you have no alternative but to go on with questions 7, 8 and 9 (possibly 10, 11 and 12) to cover every possible device that your opponent may have used to collect the information from a witness. At least, once you have prepared a set of standard questions designed to cover all known means of securing a statement from a person, you know you won't have to do it again.

Along this line I call your attention to the fact that the Pennsylvania Supreme Court recently amended a Discovery Rule which requires the production of "statements" upon request. It felt obligated to define "statement" as:

(1) A written statement signed or otherwise adopted or approved by the person making it, or

(2) A stenographic, mechanical, electrical or other recording, or a Transcript thereof, which is a substantially verbatim recital of an oral statement by the person making it and contemporaneously recorded.

You will note the specific devices mentioned in subsection (2); I assume that was put in for the benefit of Philadelphia lawyers (since it was not in the least bit necessary for the practitioners in Pittsburgh).

You will simply have to be guided by conditions existing in your jurisdiction.

But let's get back to witnesses. The principal reason that you want data about statements and tape recordings is that by the time you secure a case, get it filed and begin to invoke discovery a witness could be ill and unavailable, have moved, or have died, and thus the statement would be the only thing available to you. You can get it from opposing counsel without too much trouble, but first you have to know that he has it. Second, it's always good background information and, depending on circumstances, you might want it produced at a deposition or at trial. Once again, if you don't know that your opponent has it you'll never demand it.

II. Investigation:

1. Identify by name and address any person who was employed by (or retained by) Plaintiff (Defendant), or his counsel, or a representative of Plaintiff (Defendant), to conduct an investigation into the facts and circumstances of this case.
2. Set forth the identity of the person who retained or employed the investigator.
3. Identify the period of time during which investigation was conducted.
4. Identify by name and address all persons contacted by the investigator.
5. Identify all documents secured by the investigator.
6. State whether any Report of Investigation was filed and, if so, where a copy of same may presently be found.

While these questions are acceptable you may run into problems when you try to follow up the answers with a Request for Production of, let us say, the Investigation Report. Immediately you will be confronted with an argument that the information is privileged—having been secured at the request of counsel and for his or her benefit and guidance. The objection is valid, but sometimes you will learn that the investigation was done at the request of a third party—the insurance company involved, a relative of the Plaintiff or Defendant, or, in the case of a corporate Party, by a parent corporation or subsidiary organization. Then the claim of privilege becomes decidedly less clear and may evaporate all together.

At the very least, however, these questions will help you to learn who your adversary is talking to, what documents he is collecting, and in what period of time he has been busy investigating the case. Finally, if the investigator talked to a witness who has since died, or secured a document that is presently unavailable, then (1) you know that fact and (2) you have a strong argument for securing the witness's statement or the document from opposing counsel. Once again, if you haven't asked the question you'll never know the answer.

III. Documents:

Documents, of course, can range from photographs to maps, textbooks, construction drawings, hospital records, work records, weather reports—one could categorize a seemingly endless list of written materials. Naturally your Interrogatories will zero in on the specific type of document that is involved in your case. To this extent, at least, even form Interrogatories will have to be tailored to the situation. For illustrative purposes let us assume that you are interested in photographs of the scene of an accident. The Interrogatories would be as follows:

1. State whether (opposing party) has any photographs of the scene of this accident, whether taken before, on the day of, or after the accident involved in this case.

2. Identify:
   a) The date the photographs were taken.
   b) The person who took the photographs.
   c) The number of photographs.

3. Set forth in whose possession the photographs may presently be found.

We can now assemble a basic set of Form Interrogatories which should be useful to both Plaintiffs and Defense Counsel in almost every case:

EXAMPLE 1

BASIC AND STANDARD FORM INTERROGATORIES

1. Identify by name and address each and every person known to the (opposing party) who witnessed the accident (incident) involved in this lawsuit.

2. Identify by name and address every person known to the (opposing party) who was a witness to events immediately preceding the accident (incident) involved in this lawsuit.

3. Identify by name and address every person known to the (opposing party) who was a witness to events immediately subsequent to the accident (incident) involved in this lawsuit.

4. As to each person named in answer to Interrogatories 1–3, identify those who were either a friend or relative of the (opposing party).

5. As to each witness named in answer to Interrogatories 1–3, identify those persons from whom a written, or tape-recorded, statement

has been taken by any person or organization to the knowledge of (opposing party) or on his behalf by his counsel, insurance carrier, investigators, family or friends.

6. As to each person identified in answer to Interrogatory No. 5, set forth:

   a. The date the statement was taken;
   b. The name and address of the person taking the statement;
   c. Whether the statement is in writing or was tape-recorded;
   d. The name and address of the person who presently has possession of the statement or tape;
   e. Whether the witness was paid any money, for whatever purpose, in connection with, or relating to, the giving of the statement.

7. Identify by name and address any person who was employed by (or retained by) Plaintiff (Defendant), or his counsel, or a representative of Plaintiff (Defendant), to conduct an investigation into the facts and circumstances of this case.

8. Set forth the identity of the person who retained or employed the investigator.

9. Identify the period of time during which investigation was conducted.

10. Identify by name and address all persons contacted by the investigator.

11. Identify all documents secured by the investigator.

12. State whether any Report of Investigation was filed and, if so, where a copy of same may presently be found.

13. State whether (opposing party) has any photographs of the scene of this accident whether taken before, on the day of, or after the accident involved in this case.

14. Identify:

   a) The date the photographs were taken.
   b) The person who took the photographs.
   c) The number of photographs.

15. Set forth in whose possession the photographs may presently be found.

These Interrogatories can apply to any case—personal injury, assumpsit, landslide, divorce, etc.

However, if one is a defense attorney in a personal injury case there are additional basic questions that have applicability in every case. They all relate to the Plaintiff's medical history, work record, and bills and expenses. Example 2 represents a good set of this type of Interrogatories.

EXAMPLE 2

DEFENDANT'S BASIC INTERROGATORIES DIRECTED TO A PLAINTIFF IN A PERSONAL INJURY ACTION

1. Set forth the following information as of the date of the incident set forth in the Complaint:

a) Your exact age
b) Birthdate
c) Height
d) Weight
e) Social Security Number

2. For the past ten years set forth your various residence addresses and give the approximate dates during which you resided at each of such residences.

3. Have you ever been known by any other name? If so, set forth the name or names by which you have been known, and if you are a married woman please give your maiden name. Please set forth the date or dates when each of the names was used.

4. Identify by name and office address all physicians, osteopaths or chiropractors or other licensed medical practitioners, who have examined, treated or attended you for the conditions or injuries alleged in the Complaint.

5. As to those persons named in Answer to Interrogatory No. 4 who treated you, set forth:

a) The dates and periods during which you were under the care of each such person;
b) The nature of the treatment given;
c) As to those persons who only conducted an examination give the date of each such examination.

6. Set forth in detail all injuries sustained by you as a result of the incident referred to in the Complaint.

7. Set forth the name and address of each hospital or institution at which you received treatment on account of the injuries complained of in your Complaint and further set forth:

a) The nature of the treatment received.
b) The date or dates on or between which you were confined and/or received treatment at the institution.
c) Whether you were treated as an inpatient or an outpatient at the hospitals or other institutions.

8. Set forth the amount of the bills of each of those persons listed in Interrogatory No. 4.

9. Set forth the amount of the bills of each of the hospitals or other institutions identified in Interogatory No. 7.

10. State whether you received nursing care or household help as a result of the incident identified in the Complaint. If so, set forth the following:

a) The nature of the services rendered.
b) The name and address of each person furnishing such services.
c) The beginning and ending dates during which each of such services was rendered.
d) The rate of pay.
e) The total amount owed or paid to each person rendering service.
f) Set forth which of the persons identified herein have already been paid and which have not.
g) State which of the persons have rendered written invoices to you for services.
h) State whether any of the persons are related by blood or marriage to you or your spouse, and if so identify such persons.

11. Other than the medical bills or other bills identified in preceding Interrogatories, list every other bill incurred to date as a result of the incident set forth in the Complaint and set forth:

a) The nature or purpose of the charge.
b) The amount.
c) The name and address of the payee.

12. Were you confined to your home? If so, give the dates when such confinement began and ended.

13. If you were confined to your home as a result of the incident set forth in the Complaint, further state whether you were confined to bed at your home. If so, give the dates when such confinement began and ended.

14. Was it necessary for you as a result of this incident to purchase and wear any surgical appliances? If so, set forth:

a) The nature of the appliance.
b) Where purchased.
c) The date of purchase.
d) The cost thereof.
e) By whom ordered or prescribed.
f) The date or dates during which such appliance was worn.
g) The frequency with which it was worn during such period.

15. With regard to your claim for pain, suffering and inconvenience, set forth:

a) The nature or type or other appropriate description of the pain, suffering and inconvenience.

b) Whether you received any medication for pain and suffering and if so the identity of the medication and the dosage thereof and the frequency of application.

c) The duration of the pain, suffering and inconvenience.

16 Have you completely recovered from any of the injuries sustained in the incident alleged in your Complaint? If the answer is "yes," set forth:

a) An identification of the injuries from which you have recovered.

b) The approximate date of the recovery.

17. If you have not recovered at the time of the answering of these Interrogatories from certain of the injuries which you allege to have sustained in the incident described in your Complaint, set forth in detail those injuries from which you have not recovered.

18. State the degree of any disability to any part or parts of your body which you claim resulted from the alleged incident set forth in your Complaint. In addition, state whether such disability is claimed to be temporary or permanent in each instance.

19. During a five-year period prior to the date of the incident here involved, state whether you have ever been confined to any hospital. If the answer is "yes," set forth the following:

a) Identify the hospital by name and address.

b) Set forth the date at which you received treatment or were confined to the hospital.

c) Identify the injury, illness or condition that required the hospitalization.

d) Identify by name and address the physician who was primarily in charge of your treatment.

e) Set forth whether you have made a recovery from the condition, illness or injury that required hospitalization.

20. State whether subsequent to the date of the incident here involved, you have been confined or treated at any hospital for conditions not related to the incident involved in this lawsuit. If the answer is "yes," set forth:

a) Identify the hospital by name and address.

b) Set forth the date at which you received treatment or were confined to the hospital.

c) Identify the injury, illness or condition that required the hospitalization.

d) Identify by name and address the physician who was primarily in charge of your treatment.

e) Set forth whether you have made a recovery from the condition, illness or injury that required hospitalization.

21. Identify all physicians, chiropractors or osteopaths who have attended you for any condition during the five years prior to the date of the incident here involved and further set forth the following information:

a) The date or dates of your examination and/or treatment by said physician, osteopath or chiropractor.

b) The diagnosis of said physician, chiropractor or osteopath.

c) The nature of treatment that was required.

d) The result of the treatment that was rendered.

22. Identify any physician, osteopath or chiropractor who, between the date of the incident involved in this lawsuit and the present time, has attended you or given treatment for any condition not related to injuries received in the incident involved in this lawsuit, and further set forth:

a) The date or dates of your examination or treatment by said physician, osteopath or chiropractor.

b) The diagnosis of said physician, chiropractor or osteopath.

c) The nature of treatment that was required.

d) The result of the treatment that was rendered.

23. Have you been involved in any accident or accidents either prior to or subsequent to the incident alleged in the Complaint filed in this case? If the answer is "yes," set forth the following information:

a) The date or dates of the accidents.

b) A brief description of the accidents.

c) The identity of any other parties involved in the accidents.

d) The nature of any injuries that you sustained in the accidents.

e) The names and addresses of any hospitals or physicians who examined you or treated you as a result of any injuries you sustained in said accidents.

f) Whether you made any claim against any insurance company or other person as a result of injuries or losses sustained in such accidents.

g) The identity of the insurance company or other person against whom you made a claim and the date upon which you made the claim and whether any payment was received by you.

24. Subsequent to the incident alleged in your Complaint, have you been disabled either partially or totally as a result of sickness or accident other than any claimed disability arising from the incident involved in this lawsuit?

25. If the answer to the prior Interrogatory is "yes," set forth the following:

a) The date of such disability.

b) The nature of the disability.

c) The cause of the disability.

d) The extent of the disability.

26. Have you ever filed an application for life insurance or health and accident insurance that was rejected by the company to which you applied by reason of your health? If the answer is "yes," please set forth:

a) The date of such application.

b) The name of the company to which you applied.

c) The name and address of the insurance agent through whom you made such application.

d) The date of rejection.

e) The cause of rejection.

27. Prior to the incident complained of in this Complaint did you participate in any sports activities? If the answer is "yes," set forth the following:

a) The identity of the sport or sports.

b) Whether your participation was on an organized team basis and if so the identity of the team or league.

c) The names and addresses of the other team members with whom you played.

28. Since the incident set forth in the Complaint have you participated in the sports identified in the preceding Interrogatory? If the answer is "yes," idenify the sport and the nature and extent of your participation.

29. Set forth the degree of impairment of earning capacity which you claim resulted from the incident set forth in your Complaint. Further set forth whether such impairment is temporary or of a permanent nature.

30. If you are claiming any loss of earnings or impairment of earning capacity as a result of the incident set forth in the Complaint, set forth in detail the following:

a) The names and addresses of your employers for the ten years immediately preceding the incident and the name of your immediate supervisor in each job or position.

b) The length of time of each such employment.

c) The nature of your job or position immediately prior to the incident here involved.

d) As to each employer, the amount of your weekly, monthly or yearly earnings.

e) If self-employed, state the amount you claim as loss of earnings; your net income for the three years prior to the date of the incident here involved.

31. Identify by name and address each person or firm by whom you have been employed subsequent to the accident here involved. Further set forth:

a) The periods of such employment.

b) The nature of the duties you performed.

c) The amount of the hourly, daily, weekly or monthly income you received from such employer.

d) The name of your immediate supervisor during each period of employment.

32. Did the injuries you allegedly received from the accident here involved prevent you from attending your employment with any of the persons or firms named in your answer to the last two Interrogatories? If your answer is "yes," set forth as follows:

a) The specific dates or periods of time in each instance in which you were unable to work.

b) Your rate of pay or each period of time during which you were unable to work.

c) The total amount of lost earnings that you are claiming to date.

33. Set forth whether you received any money from any employer between the date of the happening of the accident here involved and the present time, and if so set forth:

a) The amount of money you have received.

b) An identification of the nature or purpose of the payments to you.

c) The period of time during which you have received payment from your employer.

34. State the total amount of income earned by you during each of the immediate five calendar years prior to the happening of the incident here involved.

35. State forth the total amount of income earned by you during each calendar year since the happening of the accident here involved.

36. State whether or not you are receiving any disability compensation from any source. If the answer is "yes," set forth:

a) The identity of the person making the payments.

b) The amount of the payments.

c) The nature of the payments.

d) The date the payments began.

e) Whether the payments were received by you on a weekly, monthly, or other similar basis.

37. Have you filed Federal, state or municipal income tax returns during the three years prior to the date of the accident here involved? If the answer is "yes," identify the person or organization or office with whom the returns were filed for each year.

38. Have you retained copies of the income tax returns referred to in the next preceding Interrogatory for the years involved? If so, please attach copies of those returns to the answers to these interrogatories or

attach authorizations to obtain copies of the various income tax returns that you filed.

Respectfully submitted,

_____

INTERROGATORIES FOR AN EXPERT WITNESS

Another set of Form Interrogatories that you might prepare and keep on file would be a set directed to an expert witness. In the nature of things you will have learned the identity of this person through either the answers to a previous set of interrogatories, a prior deposition, or the production of a report. Knowing that your opponent is going to use an expert, you will often find it expedient and appropriate to serve interrogatories directed to that expert. Of course this should be done prior to deposing the expert (if you intend to use that procedure) so that you have some detailed knowledge about the individual which can be of invaluable help as you begin to outline your questions for the deposition. In addition, having these answers in advance does help shorten the time required in taking the deposition although, in general, that is not a factor of great importance.

A more significant matter to be considered—and one that can be of serious concern to your client—is the desirability of utilizing interrogatories in lieu of a deposition. Here the basic consideration is the cost factor. Most attorneys worry about the cost of litigation and legitimately have to spend some time evaluating the question of cost versus gain. We don't all work in large law firms to whom money is (or appears to be) no problem, nor do we all have well-heeled clients who can finance extravagant discovery procedures. Deposing one or more expert witnesses can often qualify as an "extravagant" discovery procedure. Many times—in fact almost always— the expert will be an out-of-towner, and you will have to pay the cost of his or her transportation expenses, hotel accommodations, taxi fare or car rental, and meals, if you bring him or her to your office for a deposition. In addition, whether the witness is an out-of-towner or a local person, *every time* you are going to have to pay an expert witness fee, and every expert witness I have ever run into has a sufficient ego to believe that he or she should command a very substantial figure. Frequently this will amount to $1,000 to $2,000 per day if the witness is from out of town, and it will usually amount to $500 to $1,000 per day for an expert in your own city. If you have not paid an expert witness fee recently it might be appropriate to make a few phone calls to friends who have; you may be quite startled to learn of the going rate for architects, engineers or medical doctors who are willing to review a file, write a report, and be prepared to testify in Court. When you add up the total cost of fee plus expenses you may well learn that the expense of bringing the expert to your office for a deposition (completely aside from the deposition itself) is extremely high, and possibly prohibitive. It can easily amount to $2,000 or more. That amount of money is a significant sum if you are the one advancing the payment or you have a client who is struggling to finance the cost of his or her lawsuit.

Is the deposition worth this expense? Frequently not. It is very difficult to break down a good qualified expert in a deposition. These persons are retained because they are "pros"—they have been deposed or given testimony in court many times and are thoroughly familiar with the intricacies of legal interrogation. It is easy enough to elicit information from them in a deposition (the gist of which you can secure just as easily from their reports on a Motion to Produce or otherwise), but you're not going to easily get them to change their minds or their opinions. Such experts are well aware of the fact that they have a right to stick firmly to their opinions and will be sufficiently facile and glib to justify their beliefs. Unlike a defendant expert, the expert witness is not emotionally involved in the lawsuit (which is very important and explains why you can often "break down" the defendant expert), and this person is not the doer of the conduct complained of and which is the subject of detailed scrutiny. The expert witness is simply there to express an opinion which he or she will do—unshakably.

Under these circumstances, you might well opt in favor of Interrogatories to the expert, and frankly I would recommend this procedure. There is far less expense involved and you can get almost all the information you need. Under the Federal Rules and many State Rules the Court will determine and approve the expert's fee, and you can rest assured that the fee will be much more modest than it will be for a deposition. In my jurisdiction, for example, the fee is generally $200–$400 for a routine set of 20 interrogatories or so.

It is true that you lose some advantages by not taking a deposition—not the least of which is the ability to meet the witness and to appraise him or her as a person—but, on balance, the likely gain does not justify the cost. Interrogatories will supply all the important background material you need and will often give you ammunition for cross-examination or will provide a hint or clue as to a specific area in which you might want to cross-examine.

Under all the circumstances it is my recommendation that you serve the interrogatories upon the expert witness and let the matter rest with that. Example 3 is a basic set of questions that you can use as a guide. Obviously these are specific for a medical expert, but they are sufficiently general that by the change of a word or two they can be used for an engineer, architect, chemist, nuclear physicist or what have you. I might mention that since nearly everyone is insured these days for professional negligence or liability, questions about the insurance carrier and claims made against the expert or his company are appropriate.

EXAMPLE 3
INTERROGATORIES DIRECTED TO AN EXPERT WITNESS

1. Identify any book acknowledged by Dr. C. A. Jones as a recognized authority on the subject of Pulmonary Emboli, setting forth the name of the book, the author, the publisher and the date of publication.

2. Identify any book in the office or in the home of Dr. C. A. Jones dealing with the subject of Pulmonary Emboli and further set forth the title of the book, the author, the publishing company and the date of publication.

3. As to Dr. C. A. Jones, set forth the following:

a) The manner in which he became involved in this lawsuit.

b) Whether he is a friend of the defendant and if so:
    1. Whether he is a personal, social or professional friend of the defendant.
    2. For how long the friendship has been in existence.
    3. Whether he was contacted by the defendant to be a witness in this matter.

c) Whether Dr. Jones has performed any services for the law firm of Smith & Brown in the past, and if so set forth:
    1. Whether he has been consulted by the members of the law firm and if so the number of times in which he has been consulted.
    2. Whether he has submitted reports to the aforesaid law firm and if so the number of cases in which he has submitted reports.
    3. Whether he has ever testified for any member of the aforesaid law firm and if so the number of cases in which he has testified.

d) Whether Dr. Jones has performed any work or services of any nature whatsoever for the ABC Insurance Company and if so:
    1. The number of occasions in which he has been contacted.
    2. The number of cases in which he has done work.
    3. The number of cases in which he has testified at the instance of the aforesaid insurance company.

e) If Dr. Jones has performed services for either the law firm of Smith & Brown and/or the ABC Insurance Company set forth:
    1. The amount of his fee in each instance in which he performed services for the law firm of Smith & Brown.

2. The amount of his fee in each instance in which he performed services for the ABC Insurance company.

3. The amount of his fee in the instant case.

f) In the instant case and as to this physician set forth:

1. The date in which he was first contacted by any person acting on or behalf of the defendant or the defendant himself.

2. The number of occasions and the dates thereof in which he has consulted with the defendant, the defense attorney or any representative of the ABC Company.

3. The identity of the person or persons with whom he consulted on the dates set forth immediately above.

4. From the initial contact with defendant's attorney until the date of answers to these interrogatories, list all reports, letters or written communications that you have directed to defendant's attorney.

5. List all material that you have reviewed before arriving at the opinions expressed in your reports of April 30, 1980 and March 23, 1981.

6. With regard to your medical education and training, state:

a) The name of the medical school graduated from, the date of graduation and the nature of any honors received.

b) The name and address of the hospital where your internship was served and the dates of the internship.

c) The names and addresses of the hospitals where residency programs were served, the dates served, the type of programs, and the nature of any honors received during the programs.

d) If in the service, state the years and nature of medical work and training in the service.

e) The nature of any additional formal medical training and education and the years thereof.

7. State the nature of your professional work from the time you graduated from medical school until the present time, giving dates and titles of various positions and employment.

8. Have you been associated with any hospitals during your professional career?

9. If the answer to Interrogatory No. 8 is "yes," for each hospital, state:

a) The name and address.

b) Nature of association.

c) Dates of association.

d) The positions held.

10. Have you ever had hospital privileges suspended or revoked?

11. If the answer to Interrogatory No. 10 is "yes," for each such suspension or revocation, state:

a) Name and address of the involved hospital.

b) Whether a suspension or revocation.

c) Reason for suspension or revocation.

d) Effective dates of suspension or revocation.

12. Have you ever been denied privileges at a hospital?

13. If the answer to Interrogatory No. 12 is "yes," for each such denial of privileges, state:

a) Name and address of involved hospital.

b) Date of denial of privileges.

c) Reason for denial of privileges.

14. Have you authorized or published any articles or textbooks?

15. If the answer to Interrogatory No. 14 is "yes," for each article or textbook, state:

a) Name of articles or textbooks published and citation for publication.

b) Date of publication.

16. State the names of your medical malpractice liability insurance carriers during your professional career. For each carrier, state the dates of coverage.

17. Have you ever had any medical malpractice claims submitted against you?

18. If the answer to Interrogatory No. 17 is "yes," for each claim, state:

a) Names and address of persons or patients submitting claim.

b) Date of treatment in question.

c) Nature of claim.

d) Disposition of claim.

e) Identity of your liability insurance carrier handling the claim.

19. Have any medical malpractice actions been filed against you in arbitration or in a court of law?

20. If the answer to Interrogatory No. 19 is "yes," for each such action, state:

a) Names and address of persons or patients filing action.

b) Date of treatment in question.

c) Nature of action.

d) Disposition of action.

e) Caption indicating court or tribunal number and term.

f) Identity of your liability insurance carrier defending action.

These three sets of basic interrogatories are all you need to get started in nearly every kind of lawsuit. They represent a beginning—something upon which to build by adding the questions that are specific for your particular case. You must use your imagination and inquire for detailed information, and don't forget—ask too many questions, not too few.

HOW TO HANDLE DELAY AND STALLING ON THE PART OF YOUR OPPONENT

In every jurisdiction the time prescribed for answering interrogatories is either 20 or 30 days, and that is never enough time. In view of the realities of the situation one cannot help but wonder why the procedural rules committees of the several courts have not extended the time to 60 days, which is more reasonable. Nonetheless, they cling to the 20 and 30-day periods. Inevitably the deadline passes and the answers are not filed. Sometimes opposing counsel will call you and ask for an extension of time, but usually that does not happen. The question is: what do you do now?

One thing is certain—you have to take some action, and promptly. If you permit it to happen, months will go by while you wait for the answers and your discovery is effectively blocked. You can't go ahead with additional investigation because you don't have the names of witnesses; you can't file a motion to produce documents because you don't know what is available or who has them; you shouldn't proceed with depositions because there are too many gaps in your case, or you lack certain background information that you need in order to prepare your questions properly. In short, you're stuck.

You cannot permit this state of affairs to last very long. There are two ways to bring this matter to a head:

1. Call the other attorney and secure from him or her a firm, definite date by which the answers are to be filed. Put this in the form of a Stipulation of Counsel, have it signed and file it.

2. File a Motion to Compel Answers to Interrogatories and let the Court set a date in an Order.

Whichever procedure you adopt, the important point is that a date certain is now officially of record, and if the answers are not filed by that date you are in a position to move for sanctions.

Above all, do not rely on telephone assurances that the answers will be filed "soon," "shortly," "in a few days," or "in a little while." Someone should enshrine in Famous Last Words the phrase "I just need a little more time." If you fall for that there's a bridge in Brooklyn that I can sell you, cheap. It may be that you will get the answers—someday—but only when opposing counsel gets around to it. There's no reason for your lawsuit, upon which your livelihood depends, to be subject to the whimsical delays of your opponent. If you let him or her get away with it you have no one to blame but yourself.

HOW TO HANDLE EVASIVE ANSWERS TO YOUR QUESTIONS

First of all, be suspicious. What is he or she trying to hide? Why the evasion? Have you struck a very sensitive nerve? These must be the first thoughts to come to mind. Your suspicions may be justly amplified if most of the other questions are answered directly and concisely but only a very pertinent few contain a vague or a verbose response. The only way to handle this situation is to file an appropriate motion to compel a direct answer to your question. You will find that the average judge can read between the lines and if he or she is satisfied that the question is clear while the answer is a "masterpiece of subterfuge," your opponent will be compelled to file a new and proper answer.

In addition, be sure to note the subject matter of the question as one area in which you intend to do some probing when you take depositions. Usually the vague answer to a pertinent question sticks out like the proverbial sore thumb and invites lengthy interrogation at depositions.

CHECKLIST FOR PREPARATION OF INTERROGATORIES

1. Review the pleadings. Note the factual matters that are contested.
2. Study your investigation reports and data secured from client. Locate the gaps in the information available to you.
3. Define the issues and determine the facts you need to resolve them.
4. If appropriate, discuss the case with an expert to learn information that you might inquire about.
5. Prepare the questions specifically for the facts and issues involved in your case. Try to avoid form interrogatories.
6. Use the interrogatories primarily as an investigative tool.
7. Be sure to ask some questions that relate to key issues which, if answered favorably, can lead to a prompt settlement.
8. Ask too many questions, not too few.
9. Make certain that the answers are submitted in a timely manner.
10. Force your opponent to answer directly. Do not permit vague and evasive answers to go unchallenged.

Chapter 4

Rummaging Through a Litigant's Files: the Successful Use of Motions or Requests for Production of Documents

"Put it in writing." That age-old challenge is alive and well today, and because its admonition is so often followed much of the evidence you need will be composed of written materials. This chapter deals with the question of where to find them and how to get them.

WRITTEN MATERIAL IS ALWAYS THE VERY BEST EVIDENCE YOU CAN GET

There is no doubt that nearly every person holds to the belief that whatever is written is automatically (1) true and (2) binding on the parties. Conversely, if one is reluctant to "put it in writing," one's word is suspect and the integrity of any agreement one is trying to reach is in jeopardy. Every lawyer knows that this old canard is an exaggeration of the truth, and that every written document is not, per se, honest, accurate and important. There have been popular dissents expressed by the adage, "Figures don't lie but liars can figure," which, in a sardonic fashion, casts doubt on pages of statistics, tax returns, corporate annual reports, and some financial statements. Another warning is contained in the saying, "Believe ten percent of all you hear and fifty percent of all you read," which certainly tends to diminish the veracity of the printed word even as it elevates it above the oral statement. Nonetheless the world pays respect and obeisance to the written word in a way that it does not to a verbal statement.

MOST IMPORTANT MATTERS ARE REDUCED TO WRITING

With the possible exception of a proposal of marriage, nearly every important matter in the lives of people and businesses is reduced to writing. Some of these documents are meant to be permanent and retained—a deed, will, baptismal certificate, family portrait; others are intended to be transient and temporary—a letter, the daily newspaper, a calendar, and that picture of her current boyfriend on the desk of your teen-aged daughter. But they all represent an object that is deemed important and one that is more accurate than human memory and more truthful than the tongue of man (or woman).

As a rule, these objects are retained, in private as well as in business life—so much so that it's a standing joke about periodically "cleaning out the attic," and a whole industry has sprung up to help government and business dispose of some of its old records.

In terms of preparation of a lawsuit, it is extremely valuable to secure documentary evidence, and there are all sorts of documents that you should think about—letters, statistics, contracts, deeds, manuals, books, drawings, photographs—the list is endless. Most of the time it is the document itself that will be helpful to you, but do not forget that very often it has no value in itself, but can lead you to information that you must have. To illustrate, very simply, a hospital record, in and of itself, may not be a lot of help in ascertaining negligent conduct, but it contains the names of nurses who were on duty when the significant event occurred, and you need those names for the purposes of depositions—and the nurses' notes to give you leads in preparing your areas of inquiry.

Many of the documents you need are frequently and necessarily in the hands of your opposition. They can range from a love letter (useful in a divorce case), to business income statistics (necessary to prove a loss in a breach of contract case or to lay a foundation for punitive damages), to construction design drawings (required to prove a case of engineering negligence in a trespass case), to checks and deposit tickets (which are needed to trace funds in a fraud case). The other party has them and may not want you to see them. That is when a Motion or a Request to Produce becomes a invaluable right.

HOW DO YOU LEARN THAT THE DOCUMENTS EXIST?

There are five sources available to you in ascertaining the existence of necessary documents—your client, your investigator, depositions and interrogatories, an expert, and your own fertile imagination.

1. Interrogate Your Client Regarding Documentary Evidence

The client is your most obvious source of information. Except in an accident case where the parties met only briefly and violently, your client usually has had a significant period of contact with the opposing party and has some idea concerning the documentary evidence that does, or might, exist. Certainly that is true of a spouse, a business partner or associate, an employee of a company, and the executives of corporations. The executives at Chrysler have a pretty good idea of the kind of documents Ford keeps, and the staff at Westinghouse know pretty well the things you need that General Electric is sure to have. The same thing applies to smaller companies who are in competition with one another, or even those who complement one another. A sub-contractor to a major company knows the kinds of records that company keeps in its particular area of specialization. It's only natural; months or years of contractual dealings inevitably lead to the kind of knowledge and information you need as you begin to inquire about documents.

2. Educate Your Investigator to Be Alert Concerning Documents

The investigator spends most of his life mingling and mixing with witnesses, and as he takes his statements and gathers data, he should always be sensitive to comments about documents the other side has, or may be collecting. Thus from one witness he will learn that a defendant's insurance company took pictures of the scene of the accident on the day that it happened; while interrogating a document clerk at a hospital he will learn that the hospital records were changed, and who has the original pages; and over a friendly beer with a carpenter he will learn who, of several employees of sub-contractors, has possession of the blueprints you need. A good investigator is literally worth his weight in gold; the prime reason for this is his ability to learn more than he sets out to know and to always be alert to the miscellaneous type of data he thinks you might need.

3. Depositions and Interrogatories Are Prime Sources of Information

These discovery tools were expressly designed to help you find out "who has what." They are a natural in helping you learn of the nature and type of documents the other side possesses and the identity of the person who has them. You can have a lot of fun asking questions such as "What records do you have pertaining to . . ?"; then make sure such questions are a standard part of your repertoire. When the party mentions the types of records it has, always follow up with more questions about the precise nature of these records and in whose possession they may currently be found.

Do you remember the source of the infamous Nixon "Watergate Tapes"? It was a perfectly routine interrogation—a deposition in effect—of a relatively minor administration figure who suddenly blurted out that all conversations in the Oval Office were taped—and Leon Jaworski was on his way! That happens more often than you think. In one case I remember, a routine deposition of a nurse revealed that an Incident Report had been prepared by a hospital, followed by a more extensive internal investigation—both of which proved quite damaging to the defendants; in another case, during a deposition an engineer from a company only peripherally involved in the lawsuit mentioned that he had seen certain important documents in a report prepared by the company who was a party to the case. These things pop up most often during depositions, often as a casual statement or an afterthought, simply because it is a conversation or a dialogue. People talk without thinking sometimes and other times they throw out little asides without realizing how important they are. This is the great advantage of depositions. It hardly ever happens when you serve interrogatories. Here the answers are prepared carefully, critically reviewed, and are sometimes deliberately evasive. You will never see a slip of the tongue in Answers to Interrogatories.

4. Consult an Expert

A fourth source of information about documents is the expert whom you retain. Because of his specialized knowledge he can tell you what the other side "ought" to have and can help you prepare interrogatories in which you delve into areas you never heard of or thought of. If you are working on a serious case involving the faulty construction of a building you have to sit down with architects, structural engineers, metallurgists and other specialists who will soon have you preparing interrogatories in a language you never even heard of before and inquiring about the where-abouts of documents you didn't ever dream existed. *They* know they're out there somewhere; *you* would never have known it.

5. Use Your Own Imagination

Finally, you have to use your own imagination and experience. If a plaintiff in a personal injury action is claiming a loss of earnings or impairment of earning capacity, you just know you have to get wage records and/or income tax returns. If the lawsuit involves payment for coal delivered during a certain period of time, you know that you are going to have to get a copy of the records of the railroad or barge line that transported the coal. Certain things are obvious, though it may take a little reflection to decide just exactly how to identify what you want.

SOURCES OF INFORMATION
CONCERNING DOCUMENTS YOU NEED

1. Turn first to your client.
2. Warn your investigator to be alert regarding documentary evidence.
3. Ask questions about documents in interrogatories and depositions.
4. Go talk with an expert.
5. Use your vivid imagination.

AFTER YOU LEARN WHAT YOU WANT, AND WHO HAS IT, HOW DO YOU GET IT?

It is at this stage that the Motion or Request to Produce comes into play. Initially, it must be stated that a motion or a request applies only to the opposing party. You cannot use it if a third person, such as a bank, a hospital or an employer, has the documents. These organizations are not directly involved in the lawsuit, and your method for procuring documents from them is generally by a deposition with a subpoena duces tecum to produce records for inspection and/or copying. The discovery motion with which we are involved is directed solely to a party to the lawsuit.

USING A "REQUEST FOR PRODUCTION" RATHER THAN A MOTION

Under Rule 34 of the Federal Rules of Civil Procedure one does not file a Motion to Produce. Instead, a "Request to Produce" is served upon the other side. The Supreme Court of Pennsylvania only recently adopted a similar rule; you will have to check your own discovery rules to determine which procedure is in use in your state. The differences between a Request under the Federal Rules and a Motion under the practice of some states is quite significant. Utilizing a Request, one merely asks for the production of certain documents and the burden is cast on the opposition to object and to give good reasons for the objection. In the usual motion practice—and this may be true in your state—the burden is on the moving party to justify his (or her) demands. As you can see, the burden of sustaining one's position is distinctly opposite in the two forms of practice, and clearly the Federal procedure is slanted in favor of the one seeking the documents. It seems to me to be just one more step forward in favor of open disclosure and requiring, in effect, each side in a lawsuit to have every opportunity to learn about its case, and the position of its opponent, prior to trial. Whatever the intent, that is the result. It is to be hoped that this open disclosure further facilitates the amicable resolution of cases by settlements.

Whether called a Request or a Motion, your problem remains the same in terms of knowing what you need or want, where to seek it, how to ask for it, and how to review the documents after you have them.

For illustrative purposes let me alternate Motions and Requests to give you an idea concerning the preparation of each. A typical petition, or motion, would be the following, directed to the Defendant Hospital:

Mary Jones,	)
Plaintiff,	)
v.	) CA 12345
City Hospital,	)
Defendant.	)

MOTION TO PRODUCE DOCUMENTS

Now comes the Plaintiff by John Smith, Esquire, her attorney and does respectfully submit as follows:

1. The Plaintiff has instituted an action in Trespass against the Defendant alleging negligence in the treatment of Plaintiff during an admission of June 15-30, 1981.

2. That in order to properly prepare this case and pursuant to the provisions of Rule 4009 of the Pa. Rules of Civil Procedure, counsel for Plaintiff desires to inspect and/or copy certain correspondence, records, and manuals in the possession of Defendant.

3. That the documents requested to be produced are the following:

a) Operating Room Log for June 15, 1981;
b) Letter from Samuel Smith, Administrator, to Dr. James Brown dated July 25, 1981;
c) Incident Report dated July 23, 1981;
d) Any directive or manual utilized by the Defendant concerning Operating Room procedures and regulations as of June 15, 1981;
e) Any manual, directive, or regulations pertaining to the operation and functioning of the Emergency Room on June 8, 1981;
f) All rules, regulations, directions or manuals which relate to the summoning of additional medical and nursing personnel to the hospital in emergency situations.

4. Counsel for Plaintiff believes that his examination of the aforesaid documents is essential to the proper preparation of this lawsuit and Defendant has advised that it will not voluntarily produce them.

WHEREFORE, Your Honorable Court is respectfully requested to enter an Order directing Defendant to produce the documents, at a time convenient to counsel for the parties, for inspection and/or copying by counsel for Plaintiff.

Respectfully submitted,

_____

John Smith
Attorney for Plaintiff

In this case Plaintiff's counsel knew of the existence of the various documents by virtue of investigation (the Incident Report), a deposition (the letter to Dr. Brown), and his general knowledge of hospital policies and procedures (the Operating Room Log and Manual, and the Emergency Room Manual).

If you have served interrogatories and secured information about documents, your Motion can explicitly refer to the documents identified in the Answers to Interrogatories, in this fashion:

Caroline Black, et al.	)
Plaintiff,	)
v.	) CA 4589-1981
White Pharmaceutical	)
Co., Inc.,	)
Defendant.	)

REQUEST FOR PRODUCTION AND INSPECTION OF DOCUMENTS

To: Defendant and Paul Smith Esquire, its attorney.

Pursuant to the provisions of Rule 4003.4 and Rule 4009 of the Rules of Civil Procedure, counsel for Plaintiffs requests as follows:

1. A copy of any statement made by those persons identified in Answers to Plaintiff's Interrogatories Nos. 22 and 23.

2. To inspect and photograph the portion of the catheter referred to in Answer to Plaintiff's Interrogatory No. 1, together with the container and labels referred to in Answer to Interrogatory No. 3.

3. The written material referred to in Answer to Interrogatory No. 8.

4. The Notice of Recall referred to in Answer to Interrogatory No. 12.

5. Any written complaints, suggestions, letters, memos, or documents, received by the Product Evaluation Committee of Defendant between 1980 and 1981, from any physician relating to the catheter involved in this case.

6. A copy of any statement made by an officer of the Defendant to the public media which relates to the subject matter of this lawsuit.

7. It is requested that this material be reviewed and/or copied at the office of Defense Counsel on Tuesday, August 14, 1981, at 10:00 A.M.

Respectfully submitted,

_____

John Brown
Attorney for Plaintiff

TRY TO AVOID BEING TOO SPECIFIC

There is a constant battle raging between the person who wants a document and the person who has it, especially if it is damaging. The possessor will demand that you be extremely precise in identifying the document, and should you err in any respect which he or she can claim is significant, that person will deny that he or she has the document or will not produce the document you really want. The argument, always, is that your opponent should not have to "guess" which letter, memo, drawing, etc., you really want if there are several, even though both you and your adversary know damn good and well which document you are interested in and that the objection, or denial, is really in the nature of "games people play." Unfortunately, it's a legitimate game. Here, as in so many other areas of a lawsuit, much depends on your relationship with opposing counsel. If you get along well, if you have been fair in your past dealings with him or her, you will get the document you want. If you have been hypertechnical and obstinate in the past, you had better be precisely correct—very specific—in identifying the document you want. This is one occasion when your past can come back to haunt you.

In general, however, try to avoid being too specific in your request for documents. Quite often you honestly do not know all that your opponent has, and if you can frame your motion to include something like "all correspondence between Sam Jones and ABC Corporation during the period of April 1—May 31, 1981, pertaining to the appearance of Jones at the Broadway Theater on July 4, 1981," you are far better off than you will be if you only demand specific letters. When you get "all" the papers, you may well find some gems you never knew about. As you can realize, you could never have identified specific letters, in a Motion or Request, if you didn't even know about them! Interrogatories might have identified the letters but people make mistakes when they answer interrogatories. That's why you should always ask for *all* the documents you think the other party may have, and try to avoid specificity. A good illustration of this is one in which a building was damaged while two other buildings—one beside it and one across the street from it—were being constructed. Plaintiff's counsel consulted architects and engineers who gave him a long list of the documents they wanted to see and assured him that these would number in the hundreds! There was no alternative but to prepare a motion such as this:

IN THE COURT OF COMMON PLEAS OF ALLEGHENY
COUNTY, PENNSYLVANIA CIVIL DIVISION

Cathedral Church,	)
Plaintiff,	)
v.	) CA 89245
Universe Corporation,	)
Jones Pile Company,	)
Smith Drilling Company,	) IN TRESPASS
Brown & White	)
Architects, and ABC	)
Engineering Company,	)
Defendants.	)

MOTION FOR PRODUCTION OF DOCUMENTS
To The Honorable, The Judges Of Said Court:

And now comes counsel for the Plaintiff above named and does hereby respectfully submit as follows:

1. Interrogatories were served on Universe Corporation, the Answers to which reveal that it possesses records concerning matters essential to the trial of this case. These records were utilized in the construction of the Universe Buidling and include the following:

A. Deflection design drawings;
B. Retaining wall drawings;
C. Subsurface explorations;
D. Foundation investigation reports;
E. Test borings;
F. Subsurface studies;
G. Retaining wall studies;
H. Design drawings;
I. "As-built" foundation drawings;
J. Photographs;
K. Soil studies;
L. Blasting records.

2. The experts retained by counsel must review these records in preparation of their reports concerning the cause of the damage to Cathedral Church.

3. The records are voluminous in nature and cannot be identified specifically.

4. It is necessary that all documents in the categories mentioned in paragraph 1 be produced for inspection.

WHEREFORE, Your Honorable Court is respectfully requested to enter an Order requiring the production of the aforesaid documents for inspection by counsel for Plaintiff and his expert witnesses.

Respectfully submitted,

_____

John A. Black
Attorney For Plaintiff

Most of the time the Court will grant a Motion of this nature despite the fact that it is pretty general. However, if there is an argument you can use the occasion to force opposing counsel to tell you what data is pertinent—either in terms of dates, or category or area of construction—in such manner that even though your Order will be narrower than your motion the net result is that you zero in on the most crucial documents. That helps, because, after all, you have to read these things and it's a lot better to look at 200 pertinent sheets than at 1,000 pages of which you may pull out only 200 documents—and this, after several weary hours. Also, at the argument, be certain that you have one of your experts in the courtroom to guide you when the opposing attorney and the Court begin to try to get you to narrow the scope of your Motion.

You will find that there is a constant tug-of-war going on between attorneys in this area, the one trying to be as general as possible in his or her demands and the opposition trying to be as specific as possible in his or her response. Let your approach be that you want "everything" the other party has, or that you think they have, and therefore make your Motion or Request as all-inclusive and non-specific as you can.

WORK WITH YOUR EXPERT BEFORE YOU FILE YOUR MOTION

As an illustration I call your attention again to the material requested in the Cathedral Church case. How many trial lawyers know enough about engineering to realize that there are such things as "deflection design drawings"? An attorney, thinking about it, might have guessed that there would be "test borings" and "blasting records," but it would be the rare lawyer who, without experience, would conjure up "retaining wall studies." These are matters that are completely foreign to the ordinary lawyer but well known to a construction engineer or a soils engineer. When you get a case like this it is essential that you have lengthy meetings with persons who know the matter thoroughly and can tell you what they need to form an opinion on the subject of causation and to give testimony. Without their expertise to guide you, you will soon be hopelessly lost. Worse—in ignorance, you won't realize the important matters that you are completely missing.

When I first began handling medical malpractice cases I tried to "make do" initially by ordering only the cover sheet, discharge summary, operative reports, consultation reports and progress notes from the hospital record. A doctor-friend pointed out that I was really missing a lot by not requesting the Physician's Order Sheet, which details the doctor's instructions for the care of the patient, and that it was penny wise and pound foolish to ignore the nurses' notes and laboratory data. In short order I found that I was winning cases solely on the basis of documents that, in the past, I never even requested. My experts were finding negligence by comparing the nursing notes and the doctor's orders or by checking the progress notes against the laboratory data. This is illustrative of the type of instance in which it doesn't help much to say, "Gee, I didn't know that!"

Make it a point to consult with experts before you prepare a Motion to Produce Documents.

GO TO WHERE THE DOCUMENTS ARE LOCATED AND LOOK AT THE ORIGINALS

Funny things can happen to copies—both innocently and maliciously. As you know, you can put a blank sheet of paper over a portion of an original, make a copy, and, if it is skillfully done, one would never know that the copy was an incomplete replica of the original. Scandalous? It happens from time to time when a party to a lawsuit gets desperate or is highly emotional. That it can happen is one good reason to review the originals yourself and either have the copies made yourself or have them made while you have the original to compare.

Leaving your office and going to wherever the originals are located may be a nuisance, but it has to be done and it is worth the effort. Normally you will go to the office of the opposing party, especially where the documents are voluminous in number or bulky; otherwise you will go to the office of opposing counsel.

When you review the originals you will notice that they are clearer and much easier to read than copies, especially if there are small notations made on the page. In addition you will be able to note that some entries have been made with different colored pens, usually blue, black, or green, that do not show up on the copies. This may well raise the suspicion that they were made by different persons—or, if the handwriting is the same, at different times. Depending on the nature of your case, this discovery may be quite important. You may also observe that some writing is in pencil and some in ink—again, a matter you may not be able to discover in a copy.

These differences or variations sound trite as you read these pages, but in practice they are not. In reviewing documents it can be important to notice that a person who made all prior entries with a blue, ball-point pen suddenly makes a particularly important entry in pencil. One has a right to ask why. As you seek the answer, in a deposition or otherwise, bear in mind that you would never have known of this had you not seen the original document.

Then, there is the matter of substituted pages. Every once in awhile, when leafing through some dull-appearing, smudgy, slightly torn pages, suddenly you come across one that is bright, crisp and obviously new. Look at it. Once again you have a legitimate right to wonder, and to ask why this new page is here and what happened to the old one? It may be a perfectly innocent substitution (someone tore the old page accidentally and a new one was typed up as a substitute), or it could be a tip-off that shady and suspect activities are going on. Once again—had you not seen the original you would never have known.

Finally, if you are reviewing these documents at the place of business of a party, you will have a chance to look around and check out some aspect of the organization. Perhaps there are library shelves in the room and you can glance at the books to see if there is anything helpful. After all, if a matter of expertise is involved in the case, and a book of recognized excellence sits on a shelf, the party will be hard put to deny that the book is an authority in the field. If the book contains material that helps you, your glance paid off.

Likewise you may see other documents stored in the room—neatly indexed and identified. It's possible that, now that you've seen them and know that the party has them, they could be the subject of a new Motion to Produce. The other party is hardly in a position to say he doesn't have them! There are all sorts of things you might learn if you will force yourself to go to the other person's place of business and review the original papers. Granted that luck, good fortune, and pure chance play a role in this—still it cannot be denied that if you don't go you will never give Chance an opportunity to help you.

DON'T BE IN A HURRY WHEN YOU REVIEW DOCUMENTS—AND DON'T LET ANYONE RUSH YOU

Going through papers is a laborious process, but this is one time when the old adage applies that "if you're going to do it, do it right!" Look over every sheet of paper that you asked for and take your time when you do so.

Don't be in a hurry. It takes time to study a page and assimilate its contents and it cannot be done quickly. In like manner don't let anyone rush you, or set a time limitation. If people try to do so it can only be because they do not want you to study the papers before you. At least you can assume so.

Finally, do not engage in conversation while you're trying to review documents. An ordinary person cannot read and talk at the same time. If another person wants to converse, then either put down the papers and talk, resuming your study afterward, or ask that person to leave the room. You can't do both and do a good job at either.

REMEMBER THESE RULES
WHEN SEEKING AND REVIEWING
DOCUMENTS

1. Make your request as general as possible; try to avoid being specific.
2. Work with an expert before filing your motion.
3. Be sure to go to the place where the documents are kept.
4. Always look at original papers.
5. Do not be in a rush and never let anyone hurry your review.

USE A REQUEST, OR MOTION, TO INSPECT LAND, MACHINERY OR BUILDINGS

Very often attorneys get so terribly involved in the preparation of their cases that they spend all their time working with pleadings, discovery, and the gathering of "things" (photographs, engineering drawings, demonstrative evidence of all kinds) for presentation in a courtroom. They forget that, for their own benefit, one of the most important things for them to do is to actually go to the scene at which an event occurred. If your case involves a huge steel ladle which spilled some molten steel, maybe you'd better get into the steel mill and watch the men and machines at work. If the case involves a fire in a hotel, you had better go to that hotel and look around at the rooms, hallways, stairwells, fire extinguishers, and location of the alarm signals and sensing devices. If it involves an incident in an operating room at a hospital, possibly you ought to see that operating room and learn for yourself how the equipment and fixtures are situated in the room.

Usually these areas are strictly off limits to outsiders and the initial reaction to your informal suggestion for a visit will be a curt "no."

If these sites are important to your lawsuit, the discovery rules of every state provide some means of access for you, and the pertinent rule is nearly always tied in with the rule pertaining to discovering documents. Sometimes lawyers forget this, so it is good to be reminded of it from time to time. On-site inspection is vital to your appreciation of "what happened and why." In addition, while you are there you might view the area with the idea of possibly bringing the jury to this scene if you think it will enhance their understanding—and help your case.

Remember that a Motion to Permit Entry upon Land (or a Request for same) is an integral part of Motions to Produce Documents in most states and should be used as often as appropriate, and probably more than you do at the present time.

11 RULES TO REMEMBER REGARDING PRODUCTION OF DOCUMENTS

1. Written material has a charisma of its own in the popular mind: if it's written it is accepted as both true and binding.
2. As a practical matter most important matters are reduced to writing.
3. To learn about the types and kinds of documents that the other side has, or may have, rely upon your client, your investigator, depositions and interrogatories, consulting Experts, and your own vivid imagination.
4. Under the Federal Rules and possibly those of your State one files a Request for Production, and the burden is on the other party to object and explain his reasons for so doing; if your State relies on more traditional practice one files a Motion to Produce and the moving party has the burden of justifying the demand.
5. If there is an objection, use the argument in Court as a process to determine what your opponent has that you need, then narrow the scope of your Motion or Request.
6. Make your Request or Motion as general as possible, encompassing all documents that you can think of; avoid being too specific.
7. If the case requires expert and specialized knowledge, consult with your Expert to find out what he or she needs and what documents the other side ought to have.
8. Try to review the documents in the place that they are ordinarily kept.
9. Always look at the original documents.

10. Take your time when you review documents; do not let anyone hurry you.

11. Use a Request or Motion to secure entry on land or into a building so you can see for yourself the conditions that exist at the scene of the incident.

Chapter 5

_____

_____

Depositions: Your Most Powerful—and Versatile— Discovery Tool

PART I—PREPARATION

DEPOSITIONS DEFINED: A REMINDER ABOUT THE NATURE OF A DEPOSITION

A deposition can be briefly described as a legal procedure in which a person is summoned to your office and interrogated by you about the subject matter of the lawsuit so that you can learn some things that you don't know. That's it in a nutshell. It is the most important of the battery of discovery tools created to help you to learn more about your case.

As you might expect, there is much more involved than mentioned above:

- Reasonable notice is required in every instance.
- The Deponent, if a party to the lawsuit, will come to your office because your Civil Rules require it; if he or she is a witness, and not a party, a subpoena will have to be used to compel attendance.
- The deposition is usually held in your office, but on occasion some room in a courthouse building may be used, and at other times you will go to the office of the deponent.
- The deponent will be placed under oath, so that you may receive sworn testimony.
- The opposing lawyer must be invited to be present (note: he need not attend), and the witness is entitled to bring his or her own lawyer.
- Your interrogation may utilize leading questions and you are not restricted to the subject matter of the lawsuit; you may inquire into

areas that can lead to evidence which is within the ambit of the subject matter of the lawsuit.

- Objections are generally restricted to complaints about the form of your questions, but you may run into objections that you are inquiring into matters that cannot possibly relate to the case at hand.
- At the conclusion of the deposition, the witness has a right to read it and correct obvious errors (though not change the testimony), sign it, or waive reading and signing.
- Finally, a transcript is prepared and sent to the attorneys or filed in Court as your Civil Rules provide.

CONSIDER IT AS ESSENTIALLY A SERIOUS CONVERSATION BETWEEN YOU AND THE WITNESS

A deposition is a conversation: you ask the questions and the witness gives the answers. If you don't understand an answer or some aspect of your case you may ask for an explanation and the witness gives it. The opportunity to have this "conversation" is an extremely versatile discovery tool. It is the only discovery technique that enables you, easily, to receive an answer and then frame a new question based on that answer or to inquire into subtleties and nuances involved in the answer. In addition, you can change the subject and later return to it from a different perspective, and inquire in depth concerning a specific matter. You can utilize the tactic of surprise. It is especially helpful to subpoena documents with the witness and use the occasion to go over those documents and get a thorough understanding of them. It has all the advantages of cross-examination and more; your scope of inquiry is broader and you are not faced with objections based on technical rules of evidence.

However, there are a few cautions about approaching a deposition as a pleasant conversation:

1. TAKE CHARGE OF THE DEPOSITION

In a very literal sense, the deposition is in your hands to do with as you please. It's your baby. You are the one who is to provide direction, select the subject matter, and determine the length of time that will be involved. You set the tone of the proceeding—whether it will be casual or formal, serious or good-humored, general or detailed. Since you have this authority, use it. Don't let either the witness or another attorney usurp your prerogative in this matter.

2. DO NOT ENGAGE IN DEBATE WITH THE WITNESS

He or she is there to answer your questions, not vice-versa. You are searching the mind of the witness; the witness is not there to find out what you know.

Sometimes the informality of the setting and your initial good-natured questions mislead a witness into thinking that he, or she, can respond with questions and not with answers. If that happens, disabuse the witness of that understanding very promptly.

3. DO NOT PERMIT THE PROCEDURE TO DEGENERATE INTO AN ARGUMENT

Many times you will touch on sensitive matters that will provoke an emotional response. You must never respond to these outbursts in kind. Remember that it takes two to argue. If you will just remain calm, permit a long pause to give the witness a chance to cool off, perhaps change the subject for a few minutes, and then proceed with your interrogation in a professional manner, there will never be an argument.

4. AVOID TOO MUCH CONVIVIALITY AND IDLE CONVERSATION

It is always a good idea to put the witness at ease by engaging in a few light-hearted comments about sports, politics, or a recent humorous occasion. However, if such talk goes on for too long, it will distract the witness; what you want is serious concentration and a determined effort to recall facts. In addition, idle conversation deceives the witness into thinking the whole affair is not very important, that it can be taken lightly, and you may well encourage facetious and frivolous answers. While you want the witness to be relaxed, you certainly don't want him or her to regard the deposition as a game or merely a pleasant visit.

REMEMBER THESE CAUTIONS!

1. Be certain that you are in control of the deposition.
2. Do not engage in debate with the witness.
3. Do not permit the deposition to degenerate into an argument.
4. Avoid too much conviviality and idle conversation.

THE TRIAL LAWYER MUST TAKE THE DEPOSITION

This is the one discovery technique that must be handled exclusively by the trial lawyer. Remember that success in the preparation and trial of a lawsuit is as much as a result of intuition, judgment and "feelings," as it is of reason, logic, law and facts. The subjective nature of the matter is not often discussed by experienced trial lawyers, but it is recognized under the guise of "experience" and it is important. Accordingly, the person who is in charge of the case and who will eventually try it is the only person who should take a deposition. This will be the means by which he or she not only gets facts but also makes a judgment and appraisal of the person who testifies to the facts. Many times that instinctive feeling (often called a "gut reaction") is as important as the fact itself, and doubly so when the witness testifies to information that one doesn't particularly like, or the witness cannot remember facts that he or she should know. Don't we all recognize that sometimes "it isn't what you say but the way you say it" that is important. If the trial lawyer does not take the deposition it is obvious that he, or she, will never observe and thus have the chance to evaluate "the way" the witness says things. The lawyer will be the loser if this opportunity is missed.

Another factor that compels the presence of a trial lawyer is the requirement that some one person must know everything about the case that it is humanly possible to learn and absorb. This is for the purpose of guiding preparation, conducting settlement negotiations, and, where necessary, trying the case. It simply will not do that the person in charge of the case know only certain aspects of it, that the assistant know other information, and that a paralegal have the sole knowledge of a different aspect of the case.

On a trip to England some time ago with members of my Bar Association we were appalled to learn that under the English system the Barrister, who has to try the case, relies entirely on his Solicitor to visit the scene of an accident, crime, or other event, interview witnesses and gather documents. The Barrister goes into court with purely secondhand information. In the nature of things, he is bound to be at a tremendous disadvantage if his opponent has personal knowledge of the facts, has met with the witnesses and gathered information about the documents.

The same thing applies in taking depositions. The lawyer who is present asking the questions, thinking of new ones based on the answers given, and evaluating the witness as the deposition proceeds, is way ahead of the lawyer who relies solely on a naked transcript.

TREAT A DEPOSITION AS A MINI-TRIAL

The primary function of a lawyer in court is to interrogate witnesses. A good lawyer will not go into Court unprepared. The sole purpose of a deposition is to interrogate a witness to gain facts and opinions—and one should not begin a deposition unprepared.

First of all, an attorney should approach a deposition just as he, or she, would a trial. It should be considered a mini-trial and should be conducted with the same serious purpose and careful preparation as an actual trial would be. Thus, the attorney should review and study all materials that have been collected to date. If others have worked on some phase of the case they should be consulted to secure their thoughts and ideas with regard to the information one hopes to gain from the witness to be deposed, and the approach that might be taken with the particular witness. In addition, the investigation folder should be studied and pertinent documents or photographs extracted from it. The attorney will have to go through the Answers to Interrogatories and Answers to Requests for Admissions and note those particular ones that may be of value either because they provide essential background information or because they constitute the subject matter of the questioning of the witness to be deposed. One must also read the transcripts of prior depositions to determine whether they contain information that might be helpful during the interrogation of the proposed deponent.

Second, after the file has been reviewed, one comes to the problem of deciding the precise purpose of this deposition. This is in the category of "knowing what you are doing," and I am sorry to say that many depositions are taken when the lawyer does not know what he is doing. The result, at best, is a waste of time and nothing is gained from the interrogation; at worst, the lawyer gets tangled up in matters that don't really concern him or gets some nasty answers to his questions and his opponent's case is bolstered as a result. There is no need for this. It is your job to decide why you are taking the deposition. Are you taking it to establish a particular fact? Are you groping for documents and an explanation of them? Are you deposing a party with the intent of trying to win the case right there and then? What are you doing? A deposition has to have a purpose, goal, or destination. One cannot proceed without it. To do so is to literally grope in the dark. Remember that you are going to be asking a question of the witness and there is no hope of getting a helpful answer if you don't have a clear understanding of what you are looking for. If you are certain of your goals, your questions will be clear and direct and the witness will answer definitely and helpfully. On the other hand, if you are not sure what you are after your questions will be ambiguous, general, hazy, uncertain—and so will the answers. Having a clearly defined goal or purpose when taking the deposition is certainly one of the critical matters to be considered beforehand.

Third, an outline should be prepared to give cohesion and direction to the deposition. An outline to an attorney is like a map to a driver: it tells you where you have been, where you are, where you are going, and the alternative routes that are available to you if there is a detour. Without an outline, there is every likelihood that you are going to forget to ask questions in one or two areas that you had hoped to cover with this witness. During the deposition an answer may well lead you into an area of inquiry that you did not anticipate, and after you have interrogated the witness for ten or fifteen minutes in this new and unexpected area it is easy to forget to go over another matter that may be important, though more mundane in nature. Later you may want to kick yourself for having forgotten to ask the witness about these mundane matters—but it will be too late. This can be avoided if you will only prepare an outline. Then when you get led off onto an interesting detour and have concluded that matter to your satisfaction, you will have a guide to get you back to the main road, so to speak.

Finally, if there is any doubt about your ability to remember specific matters of importance, the actual questions should be prepared. Sometimes the exact phrasing of a question is crucial, and for those instances the questions should be written out beforehand. I have seen many excellent attorneys come to a deposition with an outline which they place on one side of their desk and many pages of prepared questions which they place to the other side. They will begin working from the outline but from time to time turn to the prepared questions and check them off as they are asked. This leads to a thorough deposition, and certainly all those present know that the lawyer is prepared and is taking the matter very seriously. It certainly gives the opposition grounds for worry if they have not prepared as diligently.

THE GOALS AND PURPOSES OF SUCCESSFUL DEPOSITIONS

Since it is critical to decide in advance the specific purpose for which you are taking the deposition, it is well to take a look at what some of those goals might be. In a broad sense, one takes a deposition for two good reasons:

1. To win the case, and
2. To gather information.

CHECKLIST

YOUR PREPARATION FOR
A GOOD DEPOSITION

1. *Review* Investigation Folder.
2. *Read* Answers to Interrogatories and Requests for Admissions. Note pertinent material.
3. *Read* Transcripts of Prior Depositions.
4. *Discuss* the case, the witness, and possible goals of the deposition with others who have worked on the case.
5. *Decide* on a specific purpose of the deposition.
6. *Prepare* an outline.
7. *Write out* the important questions you want to be sure to ask.

Most depositions are taken for the second reason—to gather information that you don't have and need. There is not enough attention given to the first reason for taking a deposition—to win the case. Naturally, this can be done conclusively only when one deposes a party to the lawsuit; it can be done indirectly however, by soliciting damning testimony from a key witness. Unfortunately, most attorneys lack faith in the possibility of winning a case by way of a deposition and do not try to do so—at least not very hard. We will discuss this at greater length in a moment.

Returning to the question of the various purposes for which depositions are taken, the phrase "to gather information" is both broad and general. It can be refined—and perhaps, in so doing, we can arrive at some goals that you have not thought of before.

Being more specific, we can delineate six principal objectives of depositions:

Objective No. 1: To win the case.

Objective No. 2: To find and prove an essential fact.

Objective No. 3: To block a defense or theory of your opponent.

Objective No. 4: To secure documents and to gather information about them.

Objective No. 5: To prove your damages for settlement purposes.

Objective No. 6: To develop facts needed to file a complaint.

Having these objectives before us, we can see that by knowing why we are taking the deposition, we can alter our preparation, attitude and approach in each instance. For example, if one is going to try to win the case, one needs a party as a deponent, the deposition will be lengthy and detailed, the attorney must prepare himself carefully and extensively, and at the deposition he must utilize every skill to go for the jugular. However, if one is deposing a witness to establish a particular fact (a weatherman, about the amount of rain on a particular day; a city engineer, about when a particular traffic light was installed) the deposition can be direct, brief, will require relatively little preparation, and can be taken in a relaxed manner. The first deposition may require several hours of time; the second, ten minutes.

There is also a difference in scheduling the various types of depositions. Usually a deposition taken to win a case will be scheduled a considerable time after a lawsuit has been filed. This is also true of a deposition taken for the purpose of proving the damages to the satisfaction of a skeptical claimsman or insurance adjuster. On the other hand, depositions taken for the purpose of discovering additional parties who might be joined in a lawsuit, or for the purpose of developing facts needed to file a complaint (where permitted), are necessarily scheduled very early in a case.

So there are important differences in timing, approach, and preparation depending upon your objective in taking the deposition. Let us look more closely at these objectives.

PART II—OBJECTIVES

OBJECTIVE NO. 1: TO WIN THE CASE

Every discovery technique has, as its ultimate goal, victory in the lawsuit, but it is only in taking a deposition that one is reasonably likely to accomplish this goal. And it can be done! If you will combine the principles of a good knowledge of the case, detailed preparation, and a diligent application of skill—all of which are within your capabilities—you can win the case in the quiet of your office by the simple and economical means of a good deposition. If you will do some hard work now, and follow the principles laid down in this book, there will be no need for five or seven days of trial, two weeks of preparation, high experts' fees, worry about witnesses not showing up in court, and legitimate concern about how your client will hold up under cross-examination or how the judge will rule on some serious questions of evidence.

Remember that to accomplish this purpose you must be deposing a party to the lawsuit—either the individual Plaintiff or Defendant, or, if it is a corporation, a senior officer whose word can bind the corporation.

Look at some illustrations of cases in which it was done.

CASE HISTORY 1. A Medical Malpractice Case: Negligently Performed Operation

The defendant, an experienced neurosurgeon, was performing a laminectomy at the L-5 level (the lower back). What he was trying to do was to cut out the spongy "shock absorber" that separates the bony vertebrae in our spinal column. A portion of this material had extruded and was pressing on a nerve. This is commonly referred to as a ruptured or herniated disc. These nerves begin at the spinal cord and then proceed through the body, and are sometimes identified by the vertebrae around and through which they pass. Thus, in this instance the doctor referred to the "L-5 nerve root." That nerve root is made up of about 15 filaments, each of which is about a millimeter thick, and while endeavoring to get past the nerve root he severed some of the filaments. The patient-plaintiff was left with a "foot drop"—a serious condition in which he cannot flex the foot up and down, and thus cannot walk without a special brace.

Now this is a common operation for a neurosurgeon, and the doctor must have performed it dozens of times.

The critical portion of the deposition is the following excerpt:

Q. All right. Proceed now with your description of the operation.

A. As I previously stated, the Kerrison was in the process of removing some bone from the lamina when a filament of the nerve was avulsed. This bone was continued to be removed beyond that part because it still had inadequate exposure to the ruptured disc. Then when the ruptured disc and the free fragment were identified, they were removed with better exposure, and then all available disc material was removed from the interspace itself. It should be noted that no spinal fluid was seen in the wound at any time during the operation, which would indicate that the dura or the sac covering the other nerves in the spinal canal were not injured. The root, after the ruptured disc and the other disc material was removed, was noted to be relaxed. It was not tight. It was felt that there was no pressure on it at that time, and the epidural vein was then bovied. It's not my procedure to use the bovy until the nerve root is adequately removed from continuity for fear of burning a nerve itself. There was no inadvertent bleeding during this procedure, and the epidural vein was bovied at the conclusion of the removal of the disc material. That concluded the operation, and a piece of Gelfoam was placed in the laminectomy defect. It was irrigated with normal saline solution, and the wound was closed with dexon suture material to the fascia and to the subcutaneous tissue. Steri-strips were applied to the skin, and a sterile dressing was applied, and the patient was returned to the recovery room in good condition.

Q. Doctor, going back to the time when you took over and were utilizing the ronguers, did you recognize that there was a danger of avulsing the nerve root?

A. There was a danger of injuring the nerve. Whether there was a danger of avulsing a nerve filament or pressing too hard against the nerve itself when you are trying to move it and stretch it, all of these things are possible during this operation.

Q. Well, in this case, did you avulse a filament?

A. Yes, sir.

Q. Did you expect that that was likely to happen at the time that you utilized the ronguers?

A. No.

★   ★   ★   ★

Q. But, I take it, you did feel that that was the more serious portion of the operation?

A. Yes. This is the most serious part, and it's a routine operation. It is the trickiest part of the operation and the most delicate part of the operation, routinely.

Q. Using reasonable medical care, is it possible to do it without avulsing a filament of the nerve root?

A. Well, I think it is the hope of every surgeon that the nerve would not be damaged in any way and, of course, that is what usually occurrs—that is, the nerve is not injured. There was nothing that was done in this particular operation that was any less careful than any other lumbar laminectomy that I have performed.

Q. And you come across nerves that are tight in other patients?

A. Certainly.

Q. And you are used to utilizing the ronguers without avulsing a filament; is that right?

A. That's correct.

Q. *So that utilizing reasonable medical care, you should be able to utilize the ronguers without avulsing the filament?*

A. *Yes, sir, that's correct.*

Those fateful words at the end won the case. Serious thought was given to moving for a Summary Judgment based on that statement but there was no need to do this; the case was settled for a very substantial sum because of the doctor's statements in the deposition.

It is worthy of note that the questions were not framed in a haphazard manner. The portion set forth above constitutes about three pages in a sixty-page deposition. The entire deposition was arranged into sections—one dealt with the doctor's background and experience, one inquired into the textbooks he used and studied from, another section related to his insurance and prior claims made against him, a fourth dealt with the hospital records, the fifth section inquired about his relations with his Resident-Assistant, the sixth with the operation itself, and a seventh section explored compliance with the doctrine of Informed Consent.

The important point is that the deposition was planned and the questions thought out in advance. Success in this case just didn't happen as a matter of luck or because the attorney happened to spontaneously think of a question.

This calls to mind a quotation I read somewhere of the very famous lawyer, Louis Nizer, who was asked about the role of luck in his success, to which he is reported to have responded something to this effect: "Oh, Lady Luck visits me all right, but somehow she always appears at 2 A.M. when I'm working in my library. She never shows up when I'm out on the golf course."

Just so in this instance. The file had been reviewed, the hospital record studied in minute detail, several chapters of a text on neurosurgery had been read, some thought had been given to the questions, and an outline was prepared. And it was all worthwhile. There was no need for a trial here—thanks to a good deposition.

OUTLINE
FOR DEPOSING AN EXPERT TO WIN THE CASE

1. *Education, Training and Experience*

   An introduction. For background only. You probably won't get anything significant from this. Touch lightly and move on.

2. *Professors and Recognized Texts in the Field*

   A former teacher might disagree with the conduct of his student.

   The texts are important. You may well find material that will prove helpful in cross-examination.

3. *Prior Claims or Lawsuits*

   This may be helpful. Don't spend too much time on it. Remember that if there are any—however the outcome—it is unsettling for the deponent to discuss them.

4. *Verify and Interrogate About Documents the Deponent Helped Prepare*

Hospital records, engineering drawings, real estate appraisals, blasting records.

This is the time to strike hard—unnerve the witness.

This is the first time to press the witness; bear down hard.

You should know these documents better than the witness does. Watch for errors.

Sharp questioning—detailed and lengthy. This is a good place to set the stage for questions that will win the case.

5. *Relations with Assistants and Subordinate Personnel*

At this point try to avoid aggressive questioning. Let the witness relax for a few moments.

Back off from tough questioning; let the witness relax.

Inquire about "Who did what?" Includes medical residents, junior attorneys, draftsmen, laboratory personnel.

Will the witness accept responsibility for their work?

To what extent did he supervise them?

6. *The Incident*

Win the case now! Come down very hard on the witness.

Win the case here and now!

Your most aggressive and adroit questioning.

Take all the time you want.

Demand admissions of liability.

Be pointed and detailed in your questions.

7. *Compliance with Statutes, Decisional Standards, Regulations, Custom in the Industry*

Don't accept "substantial compliance." What wasn't done?

Be sure you know what the standards are.

Go into detail only if there appears to be non-compliance.

CASE HISTORY 2. A Two-Vehicle Head-On Collision

In this instance the accident happened on a two-lane road, at night. There were no witnesses. The Plaintiff had no recollection of the accident. The Defendant driver had a passenger—his girlfriend—who was asleep at the time of impact. Most of the debris was slightly to the Plaintiff's side of the center line. The significant part of the deposition was substantially as follows:

Q. You picked up your girlfriend at 11:15 at her place of business, is that right?

A. Yeah.

Q. I understand she promptly went to sleep on you.

A. Yeah, she was tired.

Q. Tell me, as you drove along Blackburn Road, did you ever glance at your girlfriend to see if she was all right?

A. Yeah, a couple of times.

Q. What was her position in the front seat?

A. She was in the corner of the seat and the door and her head was against the window.

Q. You say you glanced at her to see if she was all right. How many times did you do this?

A. Two or three times.

Q. Was one of those times just before this accident?

A. Yes.

Q. Tell me, in glancing, did you ever lean toward her to check more closely on her condition?

A. Yes.

Q. How much time would this leaning over and looking at your girlfriend take?

A. A few seconds.

Q. When you are driving and you lean to the right of the seat—whether to roll up a window, check on your girlfriend or whatever reason— do you notice a tendency of your left hand to turn the steering wheel to the left?

A. Yes.

Q. As you recollect this accident, do you think you turned the steering wheel to the left when you leaned to the right to check on your girlfriend?

A. Yeah.

Needless to say, that was the end of that case.

OUTLINE
FOR DEPOSING A DRIVER IN AN AUTOMOBILE ACCIDENT CASE

1. *Training and Experience*

   General background.

Background.   Don't expect too much unless a new driver.

2. *Prior Accidents and Motor Vehicle Violations*

Touch and go.

Four or five speeding tickets, two or three prior intersection accidents might open the door to serious questioning.

3. *Conduct and Condition of Driver*

Spend a lot of time with this.

Tired? Drinking? Long day? In a hurry? In ill health? Medicated? Any physical disabilities? Any distractions—children, noise, many passengers? Disturbing conditions on road—much traffic, road surface, accident, animals?

Spend some time with this subject.

4. *Conduct and Condition of Vehicle*

Usually cautionary questions.

Brakes OK? Lights? Last inspection—any problems? Windshield wipers, steering mechanism, tires.

Unless there is an obvious defect—which you should already know about—this questioning will be cautionary in nature.

5. *Circumstances Preceding the Accident*

Step up the pace and intensity of the questions.

Now is the time to start to bear down on the witness. Detailed, aggressive questions.

What did he, or she, see? Speed. Distances. What was the witness doing? Alertness for danger signs—children playing near road, traffic ahead beginning to slow down.

6. *The Accident*

Win the case here.

Use all your skills at this point.

What did the driver do and why?

Take your time.

How could this accident have been avoided.

Try to get admissions of poor judgment, distractions or excessive speed.

Try to get the witness to draw a sketch; it is often incorrect and damning.

7. *Post-Accident Circumstances*

General questions—admissions.

Position of vehicles
Witnesses
Police and ambulance

Try to use the deponent as a condition witness to the plaintiff's injuries.

Admissions at the scene.

8. *Violations of Statutes, Regulations, Motor Vehicle Code*

Usually routine.

Be sure you know the applicable ones. Run through them.

Touch lightly and move on unless non-compliance is shown.

CASE HISTORY 3. A Medical Malpractice Case Based on a Violation of the Doctrine of Informed Consent

Most states have some form of an Informed Consent Doctrine which requires that a doctor explain to his patient the nature of an operation, its risks, and alternatives to it. The more explicit the criteria required of the doctor, the better your chances of taking a successful deposition of him on this matter. In Pennsylvania, the Doctrine was quite definite, requiring that a doctor advise a patient in four areas:

1. The nature of the operation
2. The alternatives to the operation;
3. The risks, hazards and dangers of the operation;
4. Possible long-term ill effects from the operation.

The case in point involved an enlarged prostate. There are several ways to remove the prostate, the most common being supra-pubic, retro-pubic, trans-urethal and perineal operations. In this case the doctor elected to do a retro-pubic prostatectomy. His patient was a real estate agent with no particular medical knowledge. These were some of the questions asked in the deposition of the doctor:

Q. Doctor, do you recall specifically having advised Mr. Jones of the several types of prostatectomies that can be performed?

A. Do I have a specific recollection?

Q. Yes.

A. No.

Q. Do you have a specific recollection of advising Mr. Jones that you were going to perform a retro-pubic prostatectomy?

A. No.

Q. Do you have a specific recollection of advising him why you were utilizing this type of procedure?

A. No.

Q. Do you have a specific recollection of advising him of any risks, hazards or dangers of this procedure?

A. No.

Q. Do you have a specific recollection of advising him of alternatives to this type of procedure?

A. No.

Q. Or to an operation at all, alternatives to an operation?

A. No.

Q. Do you have a specific recollection of advising Mr. Jones of the possibilities of incontinence resulting from this operation?

A. No.

Q. Is incontinence a possible result of this operation?

A. Yes.

Q. All right. Now, doctor, let me ask you just a little bit and perhaps much the same questions as regards to your general procedure with your patients, since you have no specific recollection as to Mr. Jones. Do you ordinarily sit down and discuss with your patients the nature of the operation you are going to do?

A. Yes.

Q. When do you ordinarily have this discussion in terms of the date and time of the operation?

A. I have a specific plan which is that if there is any question of prostatic surgery, I will explain this to the patient as an outpatient the very first time I come to the conclusion that it is a possibility. Then when I know things I need to know about the man, I will discuss it with him the day before his surgery or the day that I know the specific method that I am going to use.

Q. How much time do you spend with the patient in this discussion in the hospital immediately before the surgery?

A. I may spend three minutes; I may spend half an hour.

Q. What determines the amount of time you spend with the patient?

A. The questions that the patient raises.

Q. If he does not ask any questions, then you spend three minutes?

A. Possibly.

Q. All right. Doctor, tell me what you tell a patient upon whom you are going to perform a retro-pubic prostatectomy.

A. I tell him that he will have an incision in his abdomen, that the enlargement of his prostrate will be removed without entering his bladder, that he will wear a catheter through his urethra for a period of five to seven days, and that he will have a small rubber drain in his incision. He will have bottles of water irrigating his bladder for the first 24 to 48 hours, but he will be out of bed the day of the operation in most instances.

Q. Is there anything more?

A. I think that's what I tell them.

Q. I want you to search your recollection and tell me once again, can you remember anything more that you tell them? Ignoring any questions they may have, in terms of what you tell them is there anything more?

A. I don't think so.

Q. Do you habitually advise your patients upon whom you are going to do a retro-pubic prostatectomy of the alternative types of procedures that you could utilize?

A. Yes.

Q. Tell me about it.

A. I tell them this when I explain the procedures that I am going to do, because I contrast it and compare it with others.

Q. You see, previously I had asked you, after you told me what you tell them, whether there was anything more, and you said no. Now it turns out that you tell them a little bit more.

A. Then I'm sorry. I must have misunderstood you.

Q. Tell me about what you tell the patient as a matter of routine.

A. I tell him that there are three common methods that we use in prostatic surgery: that we use supra-pubic, retro-pubic and trans-urethral. We like to do trans-urethral if it is possible because we think it is a simpler operation for the patient to get over, and we hope that he can have a trans-urethral. I explain that the trans-urethral is removal of the adenoma piece by piece, without making an incision; that he will wear a catheter from three to five days following this, if this is done.

I explain to him that the supra-pubic prostatectomy is, as far as he is concerned, indistinguishable from the retro-pubic prostatectomy, except that he will have more pain if the supra-pubic prostatectomy is done, and it will always be done in case he needs vesical drainage in addition to his prostatectomy.

Q. Do you go on and explain the retro-pubic prostatectomy?

A. No, not until I decide which one he is going to have, and then I tell him in detail.

Q. I want to hear the detail, doctor.

A. I gave you the detail.

Q. As to the retro-pubic prostatectomy?

A. Yes, I did. I described the whole thing.

Q. Now, I really want you to search your recollection. Is there anything more than what you have given Mr. Smith here and stated for the record that you tell these patients, either as outpatients or inpatients on the day before operation?

A. I tell them they are going to have to sign a permit for blood.

Q. I ask you again, search your memory. Is there anything more that you routinely tell people in the position of Mr. Jones who are about to be operated on the next day, or people like Mr. Jones whom you are sending to the hospital for an eventual possible operation?

A. I can't think of anything else that I tell them routinely.

As a result of this deposition a Motion for Summary Judgment was filed and it was granted! As the law then stood it was a simple matter for the Judge to compare the testimony of the doctor with the requirements of the Informed Consent Doctrine and to conclude that the explanation failed to comply with the established standards.

These case histories are given for the sole purpose of illustrating the fact that you can win your case by taking a good deposition. This is not a rare event. It happens often—if the attorney is well prepared and knows what he is after.

IS IT ALL A MATTER OF LUCK?

Many lawyers truly believe that getting a damaging answer from a witness is simply a matter of luck or a pure mistake on the part of the witness. The argument goes that, after all, when you come down to essential questions the witness knows what you're driving at and will answer negatively, or evasively, just to protect himself, or herself. This is absolutely wrong.

To begin with the vast majority of your deponents are completely honest people. They are under oath and they will respond with a direct and candid answer even when they know they are hurting themselves.

Second, you assume too much if you believe that the average person knows what is and what is not a crucial question. Many times he or she does not know why you are asking certain questions or where you are leading him or her. Certainly the witness doesn't know the law as well as you do so that he cannot frame answers to comply with particular legal standards.

In addition, the witness will not know as much about the case as you do. Your questions can be designed around facts and ideas about which the witness has little specific knowledge even though he has some very precise information that you must have. In short, sometimes he doesn't appreciate that what he is telling you has great significance and that, inadvertently, he is, in effect, giving the case away.

Finally, deponents are nervous and do get tired. One does not begin a deposition by asking, "Were you negligent?" or, "Did you understand what you were doing when you signed this contract?" Of course one will get a "bad" answer if one goes about questioning in this fashion at that time. Crucial questions should come at the middle or near the end of a deposition, not at the beginning. Also, one does not ask blunt questions suggesting that a witness has done something wrong, stupid or foolish. Instead, one leads up to the critical questions and asks them in as innocuous a manner as possible. You may recall the words of a popular song of not long ago: "A little bit of sugar makes the medicine go down." So it goes with your questions in a deposition. The witness is put at ease, a rapport is established, routine questions are asked, and when the witness responds promptly and with candor the attorney works his way to the vital and sensitive material and then asks his questions at a time and in a manner he deems most suitable to get the desired answer.

Luck doesn't have much to do with the matter. You can get the answers you want—and need—without the help of a fickle Dame Fortune. Hard work and skill are the keys to success.

REMEMBER: SKILL, NOT LUCK DETERMINES SUCCESS IN A DEPOSITION

1. Most witnesses *will answer honestly.*
2. The average person *does not realize* what is, or is not, a crucial question.
3. The deponent *does not know the law.*
4. Usually the witness *will not know all the details* of the case that you know.
5. The witness is *nervous, gets tired, and is unaware* that you are asking a "crucial question.

OBJECTIVE NO. 2: TO FIND AND PROVE AN ESSENTIAL FACT

In every case there are a multiplicity of facts that are essential to prove in order to win the case. Naturally, you will use investigation, interrogatories, and Requests for Admissions to gather many of these. There are some facts, however, that cannot be established by these procedures and as to those you will have to take depositions. Many times—-in fact, usually—the deponent will not be the other party to the lawsuit or an officer of a litigant corporation. Also, and usually, the deponent is one who will not talk to an investigator for personal or business reasons.

A good example of this is the policeman standing on a corner who witnesses an accident but who, because of the internal rules of his department, cannot give a signed statement. He may have heard a party explain, "It was all my fault," but it is not in his report. This is a person who will have to be deposed to elicit, under oath, that most damaging statement of the party.

A second example is the traditional bank officer. You know how banks are when it comes to divulging details about their customers' accounts and transactions. They generally won't do it, or do it reluctantly and carelessly. If it is important to you to know that a specific transaction occurred on a particular day, then you will have to depose this witness.

Finally, there is the instance in which a witness is stubborn or frightened and refuses to give a statement to your investigator. This usually happens in the case of automobile accidents or other similar instances in which the witnesses are bystanders or passersby who give their name to a policeman but thereafter just don't want to get involved. A good investigator will get them to talk to him but they won't give a signed statement. This makes a deposition essential.

A typical example is the following extract. Here a former manager of one of the divisions of a corporation was suing the company for salary, bonus and other benefits that had not been fully paid. In September and October of the year he left the company he called the head of the Compensation Payment Division and inquired about payments to him and payments to others who had occupied positions similar to the one he had, and voiced his personal complaints about the whole matter. In the course of the lawsuit those telephone calls became very important. Did he make the calls? Did he apprise the head of the Compensation Payment Division of the nature of his complaints? Notice to the company was important.

Since the proposed witness would not talk to anyone about the matter, a deposition was essential.

Take a moment to consider your approach to this deposition. There are only two important elements: (1) were the calls made on certain dates and, (2) did the caller complain about specific matters?

Note the matters that *are not* important in this deposition but which most attorneys simply cannot resist asking:

- Do you care about the education of the deponent?
- Do you care about his marital status, the number of children he has and what they are doing?

- Do you care about how long the deponent was with the company or his prior work experience?
- Do you care if the witness either likes or dislikes your client?
- Do you care about anything except the two essential facts?

The answers are no, no, no, no and no.

Therefore, why go into these matters at all?

The deponent is an older, experienced man who is either going to tell the truth, "won't remember," or will simply lie about the affair. The subject matter is devoid of emotion, it does not concern either the deponent or his department. In 99 percent of these instances, either you will get the truth or the witness honestly will not remember.

So, why fool around? Get directly to the heart of the matter. This is way it went:

Q. May I have your full name, please.

A. John P. Smith.

Q. And who is your employer?

A. Jones Express Corporation.

Q. What is your present position with them?

A. Director of Compensation Payment.

Q. What are your duties, Mr. Smith?

A. In general, it's to develop corporate policies and procedures pertaining to the compensation of the exempt personnel in this company and to help the organization units in implementation of those policies and procedures.

Q. Mr. Smith, are you acquainted with Mr. Sam Roberts?

A. I've met Mr. Roberts a time or two and we talked on the phone a time or two.

Q. All right. I direct your attention, Mr. Smith, to the period of October through November, 1980, an approximate two-month period. Do you recall first of all meeting Mr. Roberts during that time span?

A. No.

Q. All right. Do you recall talking with him on the telephone during that period?

A. Yes.

Q. Right. To the best of your recollection, about when would that have been?

A. October '80, he called once. In November '80, we talked.

Q. That would be two separate occasions?

A. Correct.

Q. All right. First of all, did you make any memoranda of the phone call?

A. I took some notes, yes.

Q. Do you have them with you?

A. No.

Q. I see. As best as you can recall, what was the substance of the phone call?

A. Which one?

Q. Well, let's take the October one.

A. He said that he had been offered the job of division manager by Bob White at a salary of $38,000 a year, and he said he asked Bob for a guaranteed bonus, and he said that Bob told him he would be eligible for a salary increase at the end of six months and every month or every year, thereafter. He would be eligible for salary increase in the order of eight percent. He said that he talked to Bob several times about salary increases and got no satisfactory response and talked about bonuses and got no satisfactory answers as far as he was concerned. Then he said there were several meetings then over a period of a few months, some involving Mr. Bingham, who was then the chief executive officer, and then he became disabled and unable to work.

Q. What did Mr. Roberts say his meetings with Mr. Bingham were about?

A. The only thing he told me was Mr. Bingham said that he, Mr. Roberts, had done everything he, Mr. Bingham would have done under those circumstances in terms of running the division, phasing it out.

Q. Did he, during this conversation, mention to you any claim for bonuses and salary increases?

A. Yes, he did.

Q. And what was the reference at this time?

A. He simply referred back to our earlier conversation but not in any significant detail and wanted to know if there was anything that would be done about that.

Q. From the conversations that you had in October and November, did you gather or feel or believe that Mr. Roberts was requesting payment or submitting a claim or pressing a claim for salaries and bonuses?

A. Yes.

Q. What did you gather from your conversation as to Mr. Roberts' purpose in mentioning these things?

A. I think he was relating to me a misunderstanding between him and Mr. White.

Q. Pertaining to salaries and bonuses?

A. Yes.

Q. Now did you receive a telephone call from Mr. Roberts in November of 1980?

A. Yes, I did.

Q. What was that call about?

A. It was almost a repetition of the October one. Same subject matter.

Q. Thank you, Mr. Smith.

Note that the witness answered honestly and thoroughly, that he really gave more information than expected (it was not known that he had memoranda of the telephone calls), and all of this was accomplished in a 12-page deposition. The deposition should have taken eight pages but the attorney just had to ramble a little bit at one point.

Since the deponent is nearly always an administrative person (medical record librarian at a hospital, department head at a university or private corporation, governmental employee) who is not in any way directly involved in the case, there is no need for a lengthy deposition. The witness can be relied on to give you honest and complete responses since he or she is not personally involved and the subject matter is dispassionate in nature. Under these circumstances, you can get directly to the point. Establish the fact you need and close the record.

There are many examples of this type of deposition:

Policeman—Was the traffic light red or green for the Plaintiff (Defendant) Driver?

Air Traffic Controller—Was the airplane at the altitude and on the course its flight plan indicated?

University Department Head—What are the specific criteria for securing tenure at your school? Is homosexuality a specific disqualification?

Civil Engineer—Is there a regulation of the Department of Labor and Industry regarding the shoring up of the walls of ditches and trenches?

What does it require in the case of a trench twleve feet deep, and five feet wide and 50 feet long?

Describe the shoring you saw in the trench involved in this accident.

None of these depositions should run over ten pages. You know what you're after, you can rest assured that this witness will give it to you if he, or she, can—so get on with it.

OBJECTIVE NO. 3: BLOCKING A DEFENSE OR THEORY OF YOUR OPPONENT

After a lawsuit has been filed and some discovery has been invoked, it soon becomes obvious that your opponent may have several theories of liability or defense. As long as he is permitted to encumber you with this shotgun approach, your time and talents are going to be diverted and diluted because you must prepare for, and work on, each of the separate contingencies. This can lead to a great deal of very unnecessary work.

The best way to control this situation and to compel your opponent to settle on one or two theories is to deliberately plan to block the others by discovery—and chiefly through depositions.

Since by definition we are dealing with "theories" and your opponent is no more sure of the end result of his approach than you are, the burden is on you to take the offensive. If you do nothing, the other attorney will keep his multiple approach going to the time of trial. So—smoke him out.

If, in an automobile accident, the plaintiff takes the position that your driver was negligent in the way he handled the car and also that the brakes on the car were defective, you might depose a passenger or bystander to block negligent driving, or a mechanic who worked on the car to block the "defective brakes" approach.

In an assumpsit action for the late delivery of defective goods you might well depose the freight carrier who delivered the material to prove that the delivery was on time (or was late through no fault of your client—snowstorm, bridge out, wildcat strike), thus leaving you free to concentrate on the issue of whether the goods were defective.

As in the case of Objective No. 2, the depositions often involve neutral third parties who have no reason to do other than tell the truth and the whole truth.

Unlike those in Objective No. 2, however, such parties may have freely talked to you in detail, given signed statements—in fact cooperated in every way. You could wait to the time of trial to use them—but why? Why burden a trial, and the rest of your preparation of the case, with needless testimony. If you can satisfy your opponent, in advance, that his "theory" is going absolutely nowhere, he is going to drop it and try to get on to better things. If he won't agree to do so, your depositions can be used to support a Motion for Summary Judgment as to that aspect of the case and you'll probably win.

For a concrete illustration of this, think back about the malpractice case against the neurosurgeon mentioned earlier. A very unusual event happened there; after the operation, the neurosurgeon went away on vacation and the patient was referred to a specialist in physical rehabilitation. This doctor never talked to the neurosurgeon and of course, in the hospital record at the time, there was no reference to a severance of the filaments of the L-5 nerve root.

The other specialist then made a diagnosis of "peroneal nerve palsy." Very interesting, except that peroneal nerve palsy is quite different from a severed nerve (or nerve filaments). So is its cause. Where peroneal nerve injury immediately follows surgery, the finger of suspicion points to the O R Personnel and the charge that they failed to properly pad the patient by placing pillows at those points where the dead weight of the body will put pressure on (and damage) nerves that run close to the skin. The peroneal nerve, running along the outside of the leg near the surface of the skin, is one of those that require padding.

One might say that the plaintiff's attorney had the best of both worlds—a clear case against the hospital and against the neurosurgeon. Actually, it's a bad position to be in: one is caught in the crossfire between the two defendants and their insurance companies and two markedly different etiologies of a "foot drop." This can cause real headaches and the case will go to trial unnecessarily. Besides, the Plaintiff's attorney was sure that the neurosurgeon was correct and the physical medicine specialist was wrong. What's to be done? Before the attorney for the neurosurgeon joined the other doctor as a Third Party Defendant it was decided to take the deposition of the Rehabilitation Specialist and try to get him to admit that he was wrong. This is a little bit delicate but it can be done. Somehow, you must provide the doctor with an "out"—a good explanation. This is how it went in a 19-page deposition (again, too long). When the doctor proved cooperative, the attorney went on to discuss the problems associated with a "foot drop":

> Q. Let me show you, Doctor, a letter dated June 21, 1979, and I ask you is that your signature on the letter?
>
> A. No, that is my secretary's signature.
>
> Q. Did you dictate the letter?
>
> A. Yes.
>
> Q. And is that letter true and correct?
>
> A. Yes.

Q. Doctor, there is a diagnosis there of "left peroneal palsy." Is that your diagnosis?

A. That was Dr. Lang's diagnosis, my assistant. The other diagnosis was "status post lumbar laminectomy."

Q. Did you make a diagnosis of peroneal nerve palsy in this case?

A. I felt that he had a little more weakness than just the peroneal nerve, so I didn't feel that that was the correct diagnosis.

Q. What diagnosis do you think is correct?

A. It appears from the weakness, from one of my previous reports, the patient had more weakness in muscles that are not innervated by the peroneal nerve.

Q. What is peroneal nerve palsy?

A. Peroneal nerve palsy is impairment of the peroneal nerve and the muscles that it innervates.

Q. What causes peroneal nerve palsy?

A. Peroneal nerve palsies are most directly seen secondary to pressure.

Q. Where does the peroneal nerve run?

A. It runs from the posterior part or back part of the knee, splits off the main trunk of the sciatic nerve, splits into the peroneal nerve and the tibial nerve.

Q. So there was pressure on the right side of the leg, if one is talking about the right leg, or the left side of the leg if one is talking about the left leg. That can produce peroneal nerve palsy?

A. Yes, sir.

Q. Now, is that to be guarded against during an operation, that is, pressure on the peroneal nerve?

A. I imagine they do.

Q. And the precaution would be padding or pillowing between the extremity and a hard surface to avoid pressure. Is that correct?

A. It could be that.

Q. And lacking that padding, you could develop a peroneal nerve palsy. Is that correct?

A. If there were pressure for an extended period of time.

Q. Do you think that an hour or two hours of constant pressure would be enough to produce it?

A. That would probably give him numbness and weakness, yes.

Q. Would it produce the nerve palsy?

A. It could, yes.

Q. Doctor, you state that you don't agree with the diagnosis in that letter, Exhibit 2.

A. Yes. I think he had more than peroneal nerve palsy.

Q. Yes, you do agree or yes, you don't agree?

A. We have status post lumbar laminectomy, which I agree with.

Q. But you don't agree with the peroneal nerve palsy?

A. Yes, sir.

Q. Doctor Marks has previously testified in this case that he avulsed a filament of the L-5 nerve root? Would an avulsed filament of the L-5 nerve root produce the condition that you have observed in Mr. Grimes?

A. Well, I think that the tibial nerve or a filament from the——— there is some problem with the nerve root along the spinal cord or spinal column.

Q. Let me read from Dr. Mark's testimony, Page 34. He is referring to ———the question is: "Dr. Marks, what is causing the foot drop from which Mr. Grimes suffers?" He concludes, "The reason that he is unable to move his foot properly is because of damage to the nerve that goes to the foot." Question: "What nerve?" Answer: "That would be the L-5 root." Do you agree with that?

A. Yes.

Q. And that is the reason that Mr. Grimes is unable to move his foot properly?

A. Yes, sir.

Q. So the diagnosis of peroneal nerve palsy is incorrect, is that right?

A. Right.

As you can see, the doctor followed the questions along, changing his diagnosis, and effectively removed peroneal nerve palsy from the case.

Taking a deposition to block a theory of one's opponent should be done more often, but it's not. This seems to be difficult to explain where disadvantage lies in permitting a party to proceed with multiple theories of liability, or defense, clear up to the time of the trial when, by effective and judicious use of depositions, you can knock out one or more of these theories and concentrate on a single theory of liability or defense.

OBJECTIVE NO. 4: TO SECURE DOCUMENTS AND GATHER INFORMATION ABOUT THEM

This is an important use of depositions and, almost by definition, it usually requires a good bit of time. The first job for the attorney is to find out the answers to the question: "Who has the documents?" That is easily enough done through the use of interrogatories. The second step is to subpoena the person in charge of the documents with the requirement that that person bring the documents to your office or produce them at his office. Your state law will provide you with the correct procedure.

Once the person appears with the papers your work begins. The documents first have to be identified, and then explained and discussed. If there is a small group of documents you might have the witness identify each one for the record, initially, and then go back over them for your discussion. This becomes unworkable, however, in the case of a large number of papers. As to these, it is best to identify and interrogate as you go along.

SCAN A LOT: READ A LITTLE

If you try to read every document that is produced it will soon become ovbious that the deposition will drag on interminably. This is a waste of your time and that of everyone present. Now, admittedly, you won't know exactly what the witness will bring with him, but you must have a pretty good idea of the particular documents in which you are interested. A bank officer may bring signature cards, statements, checks and correspondence regarding a mix-up in an account at one time. You should know in advance that you are primarily interested in a few checks and the bank statements relating to those checks. Accordingly, you can scan everything else very quickly, setting aside only those documents that have special interest and reading them carefully. This will go a long way toward reducing the time involved in the deposition.

Another problem you may run into is that of the witness who knows most of what you are after but cannot answer, in detail, questions about some of the documents. This is normal and poses no problem. Just ask him to identify the person who does have the knowledge and plan to schedule that person for a deposition at a later date.

ALWAYS MAKE COPIES

Anytime you find a document that strikes you as "interesting" or "possibly helpful"—in addition to those you recognize as "necessary"—be sure to make a copy of it. It is surprising how often intuition tells you to copy a paper that seems innocuous at the time but that turns out to be important later on. You can always throw it away if you don't need it, whereas if you don't copy it you will be amazed how often you will remember that you once had the paper you now need but can't remember where you saw it or when you had it. Nonetheless, use good judgment and don't let this admonition be your justification for copying everything. Don't become a paper-collector.

INQUIRE IN DETAIL CONCERNING EVERY PERTINENT DOCUMENT

When you do uncover written material that is of value be sure that you interrogate as exhaustively as necessary about it. This is no time to be slipshod or in a hurry. This witness is the person who can tell you about the document, so ask about it.

A good illustration, necessarily shortened somewhat, is the following excerpt from a deposition of a witness subpoenaed to produce documents in a landslide case:

Q. Let me show you a group of documents that have been marked as Deposition Exhibit No. 20, and then you tell me what that is.

A. This is data related to the inspection and later, repair, of the Parkview Avenue Landslide, File No. 891011 for Bliss Township.

Q. Again, when you say "The Parkview Avenue Landslide" does that refer to the one that you previously mentioned?

A. Yes, it does.

Q. The same slide?

A. Yes, it does.

Q. What does the exhibit contain?

A. Quantity calculations, typical stabilization trench details, survey information, geometric calculations and, apparently, volumetric calculations associated with the Parkview Avenue Landslide project.

Q. Is there anything further in there?

A. Yes, it has correspondence, engineering drawings, and inspection reports.

[By Mr. De May:]

May I have the folder, please. I would like to take a moment to review these various documents.
[Mr. DeMay reviews folder-Exhibit 20.]

Q. Now, Mr. Riley, the reporter has marked this letter as Exhibit 20-A. Will you look at it please. That letter appears to be signed by Mr. James Smith. Do you know Mr. Smith?

A. Yes, I do.

Q. Is the signature appearing on Exhibit 20-A that of Mr. Smith?

A. Yes, it is.

Q. This letter questions some of the calculations that were made regarding the stabilization trench, does it not?

A. Yes, it does.

Q. The calculations are contained in a series of documents, which I will have the reporter mark as Exhibit 20-B. Look at them please; did you prepare those calculations?

A. Yes, I did.

Q. Was Mr. Smith retained by your company as an independent consultant?

A. Yes.

Q. In the letter, Exhibit 20-A, Mr. Smith obviously disagrees with some of your calculations. Let's review them item by item.

*   *   *   *   *   *   *   *   *   *

[And later, by Mr. Demay:]

Gentlemen, I would like to have copies made of the engineering drawings, Exhibits 20-D,E and F; the letter, Exhibit 20-A; and the calculations, Exhibit 20-B. There is nothing further in Exhibit 20 that I need. Mr. Brown, I will have copies made for you.

Quite obviously the important aspect of this deposition was the conflict between the engineer who made the calculations and the independent consultant. In this kind of situation you must take all the time you need to explore the matter in great detail. This could well be the crux of the lawsuit, and your careful examination of this engineer may result in your winning the case right then and there.

In this connection it is appropriate to bring up one matter about deposing persons who are specialists of one kind or another.

BE SURE THAT YOU KNOW AS MUCH AS THE WITNESS DOES ABOUT THE PRECISE MATTER UNDER DISCUSSION

This is a *must* if a deposition is to be truly effective. Gathering this knowledge is not impossible or even difficult, though it can be time-consuming. For example, you don't have to be a pilot—with a pilot's vast knowledge of flying, aerodynamics, navigation, mechanics, airplace structures, and FAA rules and regulations—to know all that can be known about one single flight maneuver that happens to be involved in your case. Similarly, in a short time, with effort, you can learn all that a medical doctor knows about the little finger of the right hand. Or, consider the proper use of high explosives; it may be an esoteric and complicated subject but if you narrow the subject matter to one explosive used under a precise set of circumstances you can match wits with any demolition expert. The key is to limit the scope of your inquiry as much as possible, read voraciously every book and article you can find on that subject, and confer with a friendly expert, absorbing all that he or she can tell you. Thus primed, you can handle any witness in a deposition. Just remember that a good definition of an expert is "one who knows a great deal about very little." Your duty is to become an expert. (As an aside, this is one of the great joys about being a trial lawyer. You learn a little bit about everything under the sun and get the opportunity to meet fascinating people. One minute, for an assumpsit case, you're trying to learn how the value of a race horse is determined and a little later, because of a botched abortion, you are studying gynecology. You will meet with a soils engineer for a landslide case, and learn the "rights" and "wrongs" of politics for a slander action. It is fascinating work, and at every step of the way you have the opportunity of becoming an expert—of learning a great deal about a very little bit of the world's affairs. It's fun, and you can be thankful you selected the law as a career.)

OBJECTIVE NO. 5: PROVING YOUR DAMAGES FOR SETTLEMENT PURPOSES

The principal obstacle in settlement negotiations is the question of liability. Perhaps it would be more apt to say that until the liability question is resolved there won't be any settlement discussion. One side has to be in the position of saying: "Look, within reason, the odds are against your winning this case. Let's talk settlement." If there is agreement on this from the other attorney, the negotiations get under way. If the damages and losses are relatively fixed as in a death case, or are easy to ascertain as in most breach of contract matters, or if they are simply not in dispute then, usually, the case settles.

There are many cases, however, in which settlement is held up because some aspect of the damages claim cannot be accepted by one side and will not be given up by the other:

1. An injured mechanic claims that despite his recovery, medically, he cannot work as long or as well as he did before the accident.

2. A self-employed building contractor suffers the loss of his business in a fire. He claims that his business would have escalated in volume during the time he spent rebuilding or reestablishing himself elsewhere.

3. A plaintiff department store claims that non-delivery of football memorabilia and trinkets caused it to lose money because it had to cancel a Super-Bowl promotion.

4. An actress claims to have lost lucrative roles due to the negligent scarring of her face by a plastic surgeon and the necessity for a new operation and a long recovery period.

The common theme running through these claims is genuine doubt, or legitimate concern, that the plaintiff did lose anything because of the event for which defendent concedes liability. Would the actress have gotten one of those juicy roles? Would any shoppers have come to the department store because of the Super-Bowl promotion? Why would the business of the building contractor have theoretically increased during the months it took him to get back into business?

These are legitimate questions for any defendant to ask. If they are not answered satisfactorily there may well be no settlement.

Unfortunately many plaintiffs rely solely on the statement of their clients and a lot of shouting to resolve the issue. Quite obviously the defendant—or his insurance company—will not accept the word of the plaintiff and as for the shouting—that's always a waste of time.

The simple solution is to take the deposition of those persons who can cast some light on the problem and bring it to a quick resolution. You will have to produce these people at trial in any event; why not do it now to convince the other side that the claim is valid and get the case settled? Take our actress—if you will depose the casting director or producer you will find out directly whether, if she were to have auditioned, she would have gotten the roles. In the case of the injured mechanic, depose his co-workers, and especially his boss, to prove that he is working at only about 60 percent of the level that he had attained before the accident. As far as the building contractor is concerned, he must belong to a trade association and the executive director of that organization can probably give you facts and figures to prove that your client lost work in one of the best six-month periods of the decade. Take his deposition!

When the opposing side holds a transcript of testimony, given under oath, and the witness having been subject to examination by his own attorney, which states that your claimant has really suffered a loss, there is no longer any good reason for denying the claim. At this juncture there can be no good argument that the Plaintiff is exaggerating the loss or that the loss cannot be proven. The transcript answers all of the questions.

In like manner if the transcript is filled with negative comments to the effect that the actress had only a slim chance to get one of the roles, or the builder overlooked the effects of a strike in the lumber industry during the months his business was closed, then it is time for the Plaintiff to reappraise his position.

Either way the settlement process is helped and an obstacle is removed from a sensible approach to the negotiations.

The key to success is the use of depositions. You must remember that sometimes you take a deposition *not to gain* facts for yourself but *to tell* facts to the other side.

CHOOSING THE CORRECT WITNESS

If your purpose is to convince a skeptical opponent that your damages are valid, you had better give a little thought to the type of person you are going to depose. If your client is the injured mechanic who claims that he cannot work as well or as long as he used to, don't bother trying to prove this through a relative or a buddy. Their comments will receive no respect. Instead, use a co-worker who is not a close friend, the foreman, and, possibly, the plant manager or division supervisor. The word of these men will be believed. If your client was the owner of a small business, try to use a competitor to testify to the great season your client was obliged to miss.

The key to success is choosing those witnesses who can be objective and knowledgeable. These are the people your adversary will be most inclined to believe and who will have the most influence with the personnel at the home office of the insurance company.

KEEP THE DEPOSITION BRIEF AND TO THE POINT

This is another instance in which you can forego miscellaneous and background questions. It matters not at all how many children the deponent has or whether he or she is married. The witness' educational background has nothing to do with the issues and it makes little difference whether he or she drives a car or is in good health. Don't ask these mundane, routine, boring, irrelevant questions that simply drag out the deposition and add to the cost (unless the reporter is a good friend who has come on hard times and needs the money). Concentrate, instead, solely on the experience of the deponent in the job or business involved in your case, his knowledge of your client, and his awareness that your client suffered the claimed loss. Probably no deposition of this kind should take more than 20 minutes unless records or statistics must be gone into.

Remember—keep it brief and to the point.

OBJECTIVE NO. 6: DEVELOPING FACTS FOR THE PURPOSE OF FILING A COMPLAINT

Many states do not permit Notice Pleading, and in those jurisdictions the Plaintiff's attorney has always been in a difficult position in terms of filing a complaint. He doesn't know enough facts to file a detailed complaint and yet there is no legal process provided wherein he can learn the facts before filing a complaint.

Some states have addressed this problem by permitting the Plaintiff's attorney to invoke discovery—and especially depositions—for the purpose of gathering the facts needed to file a Complaint.

This authorization permits the Plaintiff's attorney to engage in what is essentially a legitimate "fishing expedition." There is no other term to describe it.

The attorney knows many facts through his conferences with his client, and others by virtue of investigation. But there will be many gaps in his knowledge and these can be filled through the judicious use of depositions.

This is a salutary procedure which not only helps you to build your case but sometimes even reveals that you don't have a case and should not file a complaint at all.

There is no special technique or approach that is specific to this objective; indeed you will be taking depositions for all the reasons that have been previously discussed— i. e., to gather documents, to learn very specific facts, and even to depose the opposition and possibly win the case before you have even filed a complaint. These depositions will be for a fact-gathering purpose, and all of the admonitions previously mentioned must be applied to each deposition.

SUMMARY

It is crucial that you have a specific purpose, a goal, an objective in taking a deposition. Only then will you be able to prepare an outline and frame your questions carefully and with purpose. Take the time to analyze your case, keeping in mind that the deposition will be a waste of time unless you have the objective squarely before you.

Remember the following points:

THE SIX MAJOR OBJECTIVES OF A SUCCESSFUL DEPOSITION

1. *To Win the Case*

   This deposition must be lengthy, detailed and carefully planned. You must know every aspect of the case.

2. *To Learn Specific Facts*

   The deponent will be an objective person. Keep the deposition short and to the point. Get the information you need and quit.

3. *Blocking a Theory or Defense of Your Opponent*

   The witness may be a party or an outside observer. Take your time, know your opponent's theory well and direct your questions to knocking it out of the case.

4. *Searching for Documents and an Explanation of Them*

   Usually this is going to be laborious and time consuming. Don't rush. Make everything an exhibit, scan them quickly, question on the important one.

5. *Prove Your Damages for Settlement Purposes*

   You're trying to convince a skeptic—your opponent. Try to use objective witnesses who have no axe to grind. Get to the point. Avoid irrelevant, routine questions.

6. *To Learn Facts for the Purpose of Filing a Complaint*

   This goal is going to combine attributes of each of the five objectives outlined above.

PART III—SETTING THE SCENE

SOME HELPFUL ADVICE CONCERNING WHERE A DEPOSITION SHOULD BE TAKEN

It may come as a surprise to some to learn that the place at which a deposition is taken is a very important part of the procedure. Many lawyers feel that the setting is insignificant—a trifle. In this they are wrong. While the matter may not be monumental in nature, it *is* significant. Consider the large number of deponents—doctors, corporate officers and governmental bureaucrats—who insist that the deposition be taken in their office. The reason is simple: they are in familiar surroundings; you are not. They are lounging in their comfortable chairs while you squirm in a straight-backed one. They can lean confidently across their own desks while you are forced to apologetically clear away a corner of it on which to place your tablet. When your questions become embarrassing, or deal with sensitive subjects, they can always think of some important matter to justify excusing themselves and leaving the room for a few minutes to collect their thoughts. If they were in your office under identical circumstances, where would they go? Then there is the matter of the telephone and the secretary. Both spell interruptions and trouble. In every case the interruption is an "important" one. Strangely there are never any trivial telephone calls received during a deposition, and secretaries never interrupt for routine matters. The call is always urgent and the interruption necessary. The tip-off is when the secretary steals into the room, disrupts your questioning respectfully and whispers in a husky voice: "Doctor, it's Mrs. Jones on the phone and I really think you ought to talk to her," or, "Mr. Smith, it's Mr. White in London calling." You might damn the hypocrisy and phoniness of it all, but blame yourself first for getting into the predicament. Why did you let it happen?

Under the Civil Rules of most jurisdictions, and as a matter of practice nearly everywhere, depositions are taken in one of two places:

1. In the office of the attorney scheduling the deposition, or
2. At the courthouse of the county in which the deponent resides.

If anyone is going to be relaxed, comfortable and in friendly surroundings, let it be you; on the other hand, if the surroundings are to be strange and difficult let it be so for everyone.

Insofar as possible let the deposition be taken in your office. That is your home, so to speak, and is the place where you control the secretary, the telephone and, since for them it is an unfamiliar area, the movements of the other persons present.

Since it is your desk you can spread out your papers wherever you please and can arrange the furniture as you will.

PLAN THE SEATING ARRANGEMENT

There are certain things to remember—for example, the seating of the court reporter. That good person has to be in a position to hear well. Can you imagine anything worse than to have elicited a crucial answer only to have the reporter speak up, "I didn't get that," and then have the witness realize that he committed an error, and fudge on the answer when he repeats it? Don't let this happen. Place the reporter somewhere between you and the witness so that he or she can clearly hear both of you.

Second, place the witness directly across the desk from you if you can. If you are in a room in the courthouse, for example, don't get either too far away or too close. If the witness is immediately beside you, or very close by, a chummy atmosphere is created which makes it difficult to ask intimidating or embarrassing questions.

It's just as hard to be at the end of a 10- or 12-foot table with the witness at the other end. Here one loses contact with the witness and there is endless repetition of, "I didn't hear you" or, "What did you say?" Usually those questions are asked only to give the witness time to think of an answer, but the distance provides a convenient excuse.

The ideal is to be about four or five feet away. At this distance you are close enough to observe the witness' facial expressions for tell-tale signs of evasiveness or lying; you hear clearly and yet you are far enough away so that you are not shy about asking tough questions.

The remainder of those attending can sit almost anywhere else as long as they do not get between you and either the witness or the court reporter.

Finally, in general, no two witnesses should be in the room while the deposition of one is taken. This is not too important if they are to testify to entirely independent unrelated matters, but if, to any degree, they are to testify about the same subject matter, they must be separated.

THE "HOWs" AND "WHYs" OF ASKING QUESTIONS

The phrasing of a question is always important in the sense that the witness has to understand what you are after. It is doubly important if you are trying to force the witness to give a damaging answer. There, you have to devote some time and thought to determining how and when you are going to ask critical questions.

In most depositions, those whose objective is only to nail down a specific fact, to interrogate about documents, to prove an item of damages, or to block a defense or theory of the other side, your concern is to be clear and understandable. The questions in these depositions will come easily to you and you can follow a logical sequence of moving from fact to fact as the situation requires until you have completed your examination.

However, when you are deposing for the purpose of winning the case, or are confronted with a witness you know will be hostile, some definite skill and planning are called for. Let's think about this for a few moments:

HOW WILL YOU APPROACH THE WITNESS?

Remember that you set the tone of the deposition. You can be witty, make a pal of the witness, and get him to "confidentially but frankly" admit that he was wrong. On the other hand you can be formal, somewhat indignant, and, metaphorically, bludgeon the witness into admitting his actions were incorrect or improper. Third, you can use a pedantic approach and from the position of a teacher vis-a-vis his student secure an acknowledgment that as a matter of logic the acts of the witness were indefensible.

The keys to the selection of the appropriate attitude on your part are the personality, education and character of the witness. A frightened, nervous, uneducated witness will often succumb to very sharp, angry, direct questioning—but don't try that on the president of a substantial corporation. Most experts—architects, engineers, doctors, automobile mechanics—will respond favorably to a scholarly approach, provided you know what you are talking about and the evidence is reasonably clear that they are in the wrong. The friendly, cheerful approach works best with anyone who is calm and relaxed and with whom you can establish a rapport very quickly. Salesmen, most women, lawyers—gregarious people—fall into this category. Your task is to appraise the witness during the few minutes that you meet before the deposition begins and with your first series of questions. After you get a "feel" for the type of person you are dealing with, then you can adjust your approach to secure the most favorable responses possible.

SELECT THE RIGHT TIME TO ASK THE MOST DEVASTATING QUESTIONS

Timing is a very important element in securing answers that will win your lawsuit. They should never—well, hardly ever—be asked at the beginning of the deposition. Nearly all your crucial interrogation should be presented in the latter one-third of the deposition. The beginning questions should be used to gauge the character and personality of the witness. Then there should follow a series of questions designed to gather facts and to begin to narrow the ring. You should build up to the probing questions yet to come. At this point you will have a clear idea of the type of person you are dealing with and you can begin to needle him with some tough interrogation. Following this you might back off a little or change the subject and resume collecting facts that aren't too important. Let the witness relax and lower his guard for awhile. Then, come back strong with the sharp, decisive, rough and tough questioning. This should be about two-thirds of the way through the deposition, and literally it's a now or never situation. If you are ever going to force and secure a damaging answer, this is the time it is most likely to occur.

BE BLUNT AND FORTHRIGHT WITH YOUR CRUCIAL QUESTIONS

The general public always worries about trick questions from lawyers. If they have a place at all in legal proceedings—and that is debatable—the place is the courtroom setting. It is only there that the unintended, damaging answer, and the confusion surrounding a trick question (objections by your opponent, attempted retraction by the witness), can have their intended dramatic effect.

This doesn't work well in a deposition. There is no jury present. The testimony is going to be transcribed, and when the opposing attorney and the witness get together to review it they will be able to figure out all kinds of ways to evade, or minimize the effects of, the answer you get to a trick question. In addition—insofar as settlement is concerned—no one on the other side is going to be impressed with the answer. You are going to be met with nothing but argument about your tactics (or ethics) and there will be precious little discussion of the facts that you elicited. Don't use this technique.

If you want a solid damaging answer that you can really use either in court or for settlement purposes, then ask a blunt, direct question that will draw forth the answer. Don't be cute, be candid.

This is the time to say:

"Doctor, didn't you err when you prescribed this medication?"

"Mr. Architect, aren't your calculations mistaken regarding the strength of that steel beam?"

"Mr. Jones, isn't it true that you were looking at a sexy billboard, and not the road, when this accident happened?"

"Mr. President of ABC Corporation, since the profits of all your competitors dropped during the six months in question, isn't it reasonable to conclude that your profits would have decreased in the same period?"

You need the answers to these questions if you are to be successful, and there is no nice, easy, sugar-coated way to ask them. If you have done your job in appraising the witness and in "setting him up" for these tough questions, then you stand a very good chance of getting the answer you want. It might be that you will ask the question very quietly, or you may slip it into the general run of interrogation in a surprising manner, but, one way or the other, ask the question in a frank manner.

REMEMBER THESE CAUTIONS

1. Plan Your Approach to the Witness.
   Be a pal; or
   Be formal, tough, angry; or
   Adopt the role of a teacher vis-a-vis a student.

2. Select the Right Time to Ask Tough Questions.
   Do so in the middle or the latter portion of the procedure.
   Study the witness.
   Build up to a climax—ask sharp questions, then back off.
   Come back hard with the crucial question.

3. Let Your Critical Questions Be Blunt Ones.

   Avoid trick questions
   Don't try to sugar-coat the pill.
   Get clear, definite answers to tough, positive questions.

PART IV—SUMMARY

- A deposition is your most powerful, and versatile, discovery tool.
- You must plan it carefully—treat it as a mini-trial.
- Take charge of the deposition from the beginning.
- Know your objective in taking the deposition:
  1. To win the case.
  2. To prove an essential fact.
  3. To block a defense or theory of your opponent.
  4. To secure documents and gather information about them.
  5. To prove your damages for settlement.
  6. To develop facts needed to file a Complaint.
- Prepare an outline and write out important questions.
- Remember that a witness:
  1. Does not know the law;
  2. Does not know all the facts that you know;
  3. Is nervous, apprehensive and uncertain;
  4. Will answer honestly.
- Develop only the information you need; don't ramble.
- Take the deposition in your office.
- Watch the seating arrangement.
- Plan your questioning:
  1. Appraise the witness.
  2. Vary your approach with the character of the witness.
  3. Select the right time to ask tough questions.
  4. Make your crucial question blunt and direct ones.

If you will follow these rules you can win your cases with depositions. Alternatively, if you are not complete successful, you will develop a substantial quantity of facts and documents that will help you to win the case at trial—and a trial that can be substantially shorter in time than would otherwise be necessary.

Chapter 6

Requests for Admissions: Forcing Your Opponent to Admit Crucial Facts

Pursuant to the provisions of Rule 36 of the Federal Rules of Civil Procedure, *you* are requested to admit the following statements of fact:

1. You have not filed Requests for Admissions once in the past five years.

ANSWER:

2. You have never tried to win a case by using Requests for Admissions in conjunction with a Motion for Summary Judgment.

ANSWER:

3. You have not used Requests for Admissions to establish the authenticity of Documents.

ANSWER:

4. You have not tried to use Requests for Admissions to establish facts that will be laborious to prove at trial.

ANSWER:

Of the readers of this book, fully 95 percent will have to answer each of of those Requests with the answer "Admitted." That is wrong. It's hardly a consolation to know that you have plenty of company. The failure to use Requests for Admissions is a tribute to lethargy and a lack of imagination on the part of most lawyers. Don't go with the current—change it! Use your imagination and a little effort and with this important legal tool win your case!

Just recently a Case Report appeared in the local Legal Journal which showed how a diligent and attentive attorney won his case through the effective use of Requests for Admission combined with a Motion for Summary Judgment.

WINNING A CASE FOR THE DEFENSE

It seems that Mr. William White was involved in an automobile accident on September 23, 1981. It was his fault, and shortly thereafter claims for property damage and personal injury were filed against him. He submitted them to his insurance company and was told that the insurance had expired. Quite outraged, Mr. White sued his agent, the Crown Agency, claiming it was all their fault. The Crown Agency then joined the Foresight Insurance Company as a Third Party Defendant, alleging that they had placed the insurance with Foresight and thereafter stepped out of the picture, that Foresight was to have billed White directly, and that all notices and correspondence were between Foresight and White.

At this point the attorney for Foresight was apparently deluged by his client with all kinds of documentary proof and they wanted out of the case! The question was how to best use the information he had and the facts that he knew to be true. He could take a deposition of White but it's possible that the gentleman could evade a direct answer and leave him without anything definite with which to get out of the case. Interrogatories were not quite appropriate since they are primarily a discovery tool and he already had the facts that he needed. Instead he elected to serve these Requests for Admissions:

REQUEST FOR ADMISSIONS
DIRECTED TO WILLIAM WHITE, PLAINTIFF

AND NOW comes the defendant herein, Foresight Insurance Company, by its attorneys, Jones & Smith, P. A., and requests that the plaintiff admit to the following:

1. That on or about January 18, 1981, the plaintiff, William White, purchased through the Crown Agency a policy of insurance written by the Foresight Insurance Company which ran from January 18, 1981 until July 17, 1981.

ANSWER:

2. That the declaration sheet of said Foresight Insurance Company stated that, if renewed, each successive policy renewal period shall be six (6) calendar months.

ANSWER:

3. That the plaintiff, William White, paid to Crown Agency a sum of money sufficient to cover the six (6) month premium for the Foresight Insurance Company policy which is the subject of this lawsuit, purchased from Crown on January 18, 1981.

ANSWER:

4. That said policy, if not renewed, would terminate on July 17, 1981.

ANSWER:

5. That on June 20, 1981, Foresight Insurance Company sent to William White, 1234 Carol Drive, Pittsburgh, Pennsylvania, a notice, offering to renew the Foresight Insurance Company policy only if the required premium was paid directly to the company before the effective date of the policy which was July 17, 1981.

ANSWER:

6. That prior to July 17, 1981, William White did not pay to the Foresight Insurance Company any additional premium aside from the $190.00 paid by White to Crown in January of 1981.

ANSWER:

7. That on or before July 17, 1981, William White did not pay $223.00 to Foresight Insurance Company or any other sum of money sufficient to renew said policy from July 17, 1981 until January 17, 1982.

ANSWER;

8. That during July of 1981, the defendant, Foresight Insurance Company, sent to and William White received a termination notice indicating that said policy had been cancelled for lack of payment.

ANSWER:

9. That in August of 1981, Foresight Insurance Company sent to and William White received a final termination notice indicating that the policy had been cancelled for nonpayment of premium on July 17, 1981.

ANSWER:

> Respectfully Submitted,
>
> JONES & SMITH, P.A.
> By_____
> Steve Smith, Esquire
> Attorney for Foresight Insurance
> Company

Upon receipt of these Requests, Plaintiff's Counsel apparently realized he had a problem. He did not answer the Requests within the original time period or an extension thereof. So the defense attorney filed a Motion for Summary Judgment arguing that the Requests must be accepted as admitted and that based on those facts Foresight Insurance Company was entitled to the Summary Judgment.

The Court agreed. It began its Opinion by stating "the facts as admitted on the record are that" and then quoted from the Requests for Admissions. It then concluded with the statement: "Based upon those undisputed facts, there is no question for the finder of fact and Summary Judgment is appropriate in this action."

Chalk up a winner for a good defense attorney and his sagacious use of Requests for Admissions.

WINNING A CASE FOR THE PLAINTIFF

Another case in which Requests for Admissions were effectively used by a Plaintiff's attorney was one in which a woman went to the hospital for a hysterectomy. Prior to the operation she was given a routine injection in the left arm. Almost immediately a large reddened area appeared at the injection site. It was noted but ignored by the hospital personnel. Suffice it to say that eventually the area became necrotic and an operation had to be performed which left her with a saucer-shaped depression in the upper portion of her arm. When her lawyer conducted an investigation he learned that the pre-operative injection consisted of three medications—Demerol, Atropine, and Vistaril. If you will check the Physicians Desk Reference (PDR), which every attorney who handles medical malpractice cases must have, you will note that Vistaril is a powerful and somewhat dangerous drug. It must be given intramuscularly; if given just under the skin (subcutaneously) real troubles can occur. In the case in point, the lady had troubles.

Now at this stage consider the position of the Plaintiff's attorney. The hospital records established the injection of the drug; the PDR (a standard, recognized text) gave him his proof as to the dangers associated with the use of the drug; the obvious condition of the client plus the subsequent hospital records gave him the required proof regarding the end result.

All that was left was to prove the requisite knowledge on the part of the Defendant hospital and its personnel. One might utilize Interrogatories and a deposition of the nurse involved. The interrogatories, however, give the opposition a chance to be vague and indefinite and, as to the deposition, the nurse will either not remember the incident or will insist that she did everything right. Then the Defendant, or the insurance company, will argue that they have to "take her word" and will balk at settlement. Better to leave certain things off the record. The neat, tidy way to handle this situation is to serve Requests for Admissions and that was done:

REQUESTS FOR ADMISSIONS

Pursuant to the provisions of Rule 4104 of the Rules of Civil Procedure the Defendant is requested to admit the following:

1. On April 27, 1981 Jean Riley was a patient in the State University Hospital.

ANSWER: Admitted.

2. She was operated upon on that date.

ANSWER: Admitted.

3. At 9:30 A.M. on that day she was given a preoperative injection.

ANSWER: Admitted.

4. This preoperative injection consisted of three medications, including Vistaril.

ANSWER: Admitted.

5. At 10:45 A.M. a large reddened area was noted at the site of the preoperative injection.

ANSWER: Denied. The operative record indicates "large reddened area, left forearm (site of pre-op injection) noted." The site of the preoperative injection was not, however, the left forearm, but rather the left deltoid area.

6. This defendant knows that Vistaril can cause severe irritation and local reaction which can lead to skin necrosis.

ANSWER: Defendant is a corporation and therefore has no "knowledge" other than the knowledge of its agents or employees. Defendant therefore objects to this request for admission because it is not directed to the knowledge of any specific agent or employee of the defendant.

7. Proper nursing procedure requires that Vistaril be injected intramuscularly.

ANSWER: It is admitted that P.D.R. instructions indicate that Vistaril is to be administered intramuscularly. It is denied, however, that non-intramuscular injections of Vistaril necessarily imply improper nursing procedure.

8. Vistaril, given subcutaneously, causes irritation and local reaction which can lead to skin necrosis.

ANSWER: Defendant is a corporation and therefore has no "knowledge" other than the knowledge of its agents or employees. Defendant therefore objects to this request for admission because it is not directed to the knowledge of any specific agent or employee of the defendant.

Note the evasive answers to questions 6 and 8. You will run into this from time to time. There is no alternative but to force the issue by filing a Motion to Compel Answers which, in nearly every instance, will be granted and the answers will come back "admitted."

With this information in hand, what is left to try in Court? The nurse could testify until she is blue in the face that she definitely gave the shot intramuscularly but the facts clearly show that she did not. It is practically unheard of to give Vistaril intramuscularly and get a reaction like this. How would it extravasate back to the skin? It had to have been given—probably hurriedly and negligently—subcutaneously.

Fortunately the defense attorney did not have to face the sworn testimony of the nurse via a deposition that she had acted properly so there was no formal impediment on the record (which can sometimes be embarrassing) to his candidly admitting that the nurse had to have made an error here. Thus a very good settlement was effected—and this within a relatively short time after the lawsuit was filed. Think of the savings in time, energy and money! There was no trial here, and no waiting for two years or so to conclude the case. It took the Plaintiff's attorney a matter of hours to review the records and the PDR, to confer with an expert, to prepare the Requests for Admissions, and to negotiate with the defense attorney. Then the case was over and successfully concluded.

These two illustrations, from both the Plaintiff's and the Defendant's point of view, show what you can do with this discovery tool. To be sure, you cannot use it effectively in every case. It has its own limitations. But you should not forget about it entirely as so many attorneys seem to do. Let us consider the manner in which you can best utilize this technique.

USE REQUESTS FOR ADMISSION WHEN:

1. You can *nail down* specific crucial facts and you intend to follow with a Motion for Summary Judgment.
2. You have *numerous documents* to be admitted into evidence and want the other side to admit their authenticity.
3. You want to *establish certain facts* that you believe to be uncontested but which would be laborious to prove at trial.

USING REQUESTS FOR ADMISSIONS TO WIN YOUR CASE

This can be done, and the effort should be made much more often than it is at present. Requests for Admissions are really in the category of a "forgotten" discovery technique. You should begin to think of using this device to win your case most often in Assumpsit cases, Decedent's Estates matters, Land Condemnation cases, or those involving disputes over title to land and other cases in which dates, statistics, and documents will be the primary basis for winning rather than Trespass, Custody, Support, Divorce, or similar cases in which there are wildly divergent concepts of facts and inferences to be drawn from them. Admittedly you cannot often use Requests to win a case but you have to be aware of the fact that it can be done and you have to pick and choose the case in which you attempt it. Usually these will be cases in which there is little opinion or judgment involved and those cases in which the facts, if developed and organized properly, can push your opponent into a corner from which there is no escape. Those kinds of situations most usually occur in Assumpsit cases wherein your opponent can be forced to admit certain inescapable facts because they are a matter of record somewhere or they are contained in pertinent documents. For example, one cannot quarrel, easily, about the postmark on a letter evidencing the date of mailing, monthly production figures of a foundry, a report submitted under OSHA, an itemized income tax return, employments records or a Schedule of Benefits payable under an insurance policy. Where these facts are crucial, and especially when they come from your opponent's own records by way of a Motion for Production, you had better look carefully at your case to see whether you can set up your opponent for the "coup de grace" by preparing a Request for Admissions to be followed by a Motion for Summary Judgment.

You know that many lawsuits for breach of contract exist solely because one party stubbornly refuses to look at the facts as they are rather than as he or she remembers, or thinks, them to be, and rationalizes his or her position by all manner of emotional and irrelevant justifications for refusing to pay or perform under a contract. Sometimes the client is trying to "sneak one through"; usually the client is just angry at the opposition for some irrelevant reason and refuses to abide by the terms of the contract; and finally, some clients are simply forgetful or insist, "I never received that paper in time," or "we never made that much money." If you have the data—either directly from your client or developed through other Discovery techniques—then you can prepare Requests for Admissions that go to the very heart of the case. What is the other attorney to do? He must answer, won't let the client lie about the matter, and when he confronts him or her with the facts, that person has no alternative but to admit them. This client may still insist upon placing a peculiar interpretation on these facts, but once you have the answers you can file your Motion for Summary Judgment and more times than not you will get it because the Court will construe the facts in their ordinary sense.

More usually, however, when a recalcitrant client is forced to answer the Requests—and face the facts in their starkest form—he or she will, however reluctantly, begin to be more realistic and you will be on your way to a good settlement.

Consider a case for a commission on certain insurance premiums. The arrangement was that as a bank gave loans to its customers they were to be insured through the defendant insurance company. Plaintiff, in the contract, was named General Agent for the insurance company and was authorized to solicit credit insurance on the lines of debtors of the bank. It was a great arrangement for the General Agent, who worked aggressively with the bank and began to make a lot of money. When the plan began to work smoothly and profitably, the insurance company decided to cut out the General Agent and deal directly with the bank. There was a lot of money involved here and the General Agent filed suit. The Insurance company tried to challenge the contract (by evidence outside its plain terms) and also relied on a certain Letter of Termination it sent to the General Agent which was never accepted by him. By means of normal discovery procedures the pertinent contract (and two older ones Defendant kept talking about) were secured, the Defendant's copy of the Letter of Termination was produced, and gross sales during the relevant time period was secured. With these in hand, counsel for Plaintiff then prepared the following Requests for Admissions:

IN THE DISTRICT COURT OF THE UNITED STATES FOR THE WESTERN DISTRICT OF PENNSYLVANIA

CAPITAL INSURANCE AGENCY, INC.)
    a Pennsylvania Corporation   )
           Plaintiff,   )
              v.   ) Civil Action No. 81-1234
WESTERN NATIONAL INSURANCE)
COMPANY, a Deleware Corporation)
         Defendant.   )

REQUESTS FOR ADMISSIONS

To: WESTERN NATIONAL INSURANCE COMPANY, Defendant, and John P. Smith, Esquire, its attorney:

You are hereby requested, pursuant to Rule 36 of the Federal Rules of Civil Procedure, to admit, for the purposes of this lawsuit only, the truth of the following statements:

1. Plaintiff's Exhibits 1, 2, and 3 attached to Plaintiff's Complaint constitute the Contracts between the Parties hereto during the period December 1, 1978, and the present time.

ANSWER: Admitted.

2. Plaintiff's Exhibit 3 constitutes the Contract that is the subject matter of this lawsuit.

ANSWER: Admitted.

3. That Exhibit 3 is the only Contract in effect between the parties hereto during the period of October 1, 1979 (its effective date) and the present time.

ANSWER: Admitted.

4. That between October 1, 1979 and April 1, 1980, Defendant paid commissions to Plaintiff on all Life Insurance Policies and all Disability Insurance Policies written through the Southwest Pennsylvania Bank.

ANSWER: Admitted.

5. That the letter which is set forth below (Exhibit 4) is the only letter sent by Defendant or Southwest Pennsylvania Bank to Plaintiff relating to the subject of termination of the contract of October 1, 1979.

EXHIBIT 4

WESTERN NATIONAL INSURANCE COMPANY
784 McKenzie Avenue
Wilmington, Deleware

Capital Insurance Agency, Inc.
567 Elgin Avenue
Pittsburgh, Pa.

April 8, 1980

GENTLEMEN:

On October 1, 1979, a General Agent's Contract was entered into between Western National Insurance Company and Capital Insurance Agency, Inc., wherein Capital Insurance Agency, Inc., was granted as General Agent to solicit Credit Insurance on the lives of debtors of Southwest Pennsylvania Bank, Pittsburgh, Pa.

Under the provisions of its paragraph seven, written notice is hereby given that by mutual consent this contract is to be terminated as of the first day of April, 1980.

Your written acknowledgment of this termination by signature and return of one copy of this letter will be sincerely appreciated.

Sincerely,

_____

J. R. Smith

JRS/cb
Attachment
Acknowledged by:_____
Capital Insurance, Inc.

ANSWER: Admitted.

6. The Plaintiff never signed, nor returned, that letter to Defendant, nor any copy thereof.

ANSWER: Admitted.

7. That Plaintiff has been paid no commissions by Defendant since April 1, 1980.

ANSWER: Admitted.

8. That Defendant, since April 1, 1980, has grossed a total of $1,285,942.80 in insurance premiums on life insurance policies and disability policies written through Southwest Pennsylvania Bank.

ANSWER: Admitted

Respectfully Submitted,

_____

Attorney for Plaintiff

I am sure the defense attorney knew the game was over as soon as he sat down with his client to prepare the answers. It was clear that Exhibit 3 was the only pertinent Contract, that it required the General Agent's consent to terminate, and that the Letter of Termination (Exhibit 4) was never signed or accepted in any way by the Plaintiff. The Insurance Company could yell, scream, be stubborn, feel "robbed," shout defiance—in short, pull any tantrum it pleased—but the facts were there staring it in the face. There was no place to go. For the Plaintiff it was simply a matter of computing his percentage of $1,285,942.80 and deciding how much of a break, if any, he wanted to give the Defendant in a settlement, and that is what happened.

Once again—there was no trial required, no lengthy delay, and no endless work on the part of counsel for Plaintiff. But it did take a conscious recognition of the fact that this case could be won with Requests for Admissions. That is the area in which many attorneys fail; they lack the "conscious recognition" of what can be done with Requests for Admission and when to use them. You should permanently lock in the back of your mind the realization that you can win a case with Requests for Admissions and constantly be on the lookout for those cases in which this device can be effectively used. They work! But you have to know your case, analyze it carefully, and decide whether this particular case is one that can be brought to a quick conclusion by this method.

USE REQUESTS FOR ADMISSIONS TO ESTABLISH THE AUTHENTICITY OF RECORDS

In this day and age we are all getting more cases that involve large numbers of exhibits. These cases are usually class-action matters, Civil Rights cases, Antitrust actions, Assumpsit cases, and even some Support matters. Anytime one gets involved in a case in which there is a multiplicity of parties, or a case involving records of an industrial company or a financial institution or a governmental unit, one is going to have 101 pieces of paper (or 1001) that have to be admitted into evidence. It's true that at some point you could sit down with your adversary and prepare a Stipulation Concerning Exhibits, but that gets cumbersome since it means trying to arrange a meeting and toting a box of papers to his or her office and then reviewing them one by one and making a decision at that time. More importantly, perhaps, many attorneys (including your adversary?) begin to get nervous and feel that they are being put on the spot if you ask them to stipulate to the exhibits. If they agree to something and it later turns out badly for some reason, they are the ones who will catch it from the client. It is far better, in this view, to serve a Request for Admissions, attach the documents to the Request (or deliver them separately if they are bulky), and then the attorney can refer them to the client for answer. In that way it is the client who signs the Answers saying that he agrees with the Request, and the documents can be reviewed in a more leisurely manner. And, if the client obstinately refuses to admit the authenticity (or whatever) of the documents and, later, the Court imposes sanctions under the Rule, the attorney cannot be blamed for the problem.

As you can see, the choice of routes for you to follow is often controlled by the self-confidence of your adversary and his or her relationship and modus operandi with his or her client.

At any rate if you will adopt this procedure you will find that a large number of your documents will definitely be acknowledged as authentic, thus saving a considerable amount of time at trial. As to the remainder, you might be able to meet with counsel, explain your purposes in using the document, and get him to agree to some of them, and only a small balance will be left to be proven at trial.

This is a great time saver. It need not be the kind of thing you utilize solely when you have a host of papers; you can use it effectively even with a small number of exhibits and should get into the habit of doing so. Even if your documents consist only of a weather report, police report, hospital record and a few bills, it is advantageous to get the opposing party committed to their authenticity at an early stage so that there is one less matter for you to worry about. As you well know, in the preparation of a lawsuit there are so many things to do—research, discovery, directing investigation, meeting with clients and witnesses, fighting with doctors and other experts to get their reports, dealing with opposing attorneys—that the sooner you can get one matter firmly and finally in place the better off you are. Which leads to another use of Requests for Admissions.

USE REQUESTS FOR ADMISSIONS TO ESTABLISH NECESSARY BUT UNDISPUTED FACTS

In every case there are literally a host of facts which might be described as "nuisance but necessary" cluttering up your file and your mind. Most of the time we tend not to do much about them, figuring that at trial time we will get the opposing counsel to stipulate to them or just have any old witness testify to them. Most of the time that's just the way it happens, but once in a while we forget, opposing counsel suddenly gets obnoxious (maybe because you just offended him), or the Court gets hypertechnical—and bam! you find yourself in the embarrassing position of not being able to prove some little, but important, fact. Sure, usually you can wriggle out of this jam but why get into it in the first place? There are all kinds of facts like these:

- The kind of car the opposing party was driving.
- The time an operation began and ended.
- The last date an airplane engine was inspected.
- The Social Security number of a decedent.
- The quantity of goods delivered under a prior contract.
- The Civil Action Number and date of filing of a related lawsuit.
- The price of a particular stock on the New York Stock Exchange on a certain date.
- The date a deed was filed.

I'm sure you will agree that there are dozens of facts of a similar nature that you usually don't go to any great effort to prove. Yet they have to nag at you, and I consider that one reason so many lawyers suffer from ulcers is that they don't nail these things down once and for all. That, and procrastination. It's far better—and it will ease your mind—to list these facts in an orderly manner, prepare a Request for Admissions as to them, get the other side to admit them, and then you can forget about them. It's that much less to worry about. At trial time all you have to do is to pick up the document and read the facts into the record.

A FEW "DONT'S" REGARDING REQUESTS FOR ADMISSIONS

There are certain things that this legal tool cannot do for you. It is not a good investigative device, for example. You can't easily use Requests to search for facts or to "snoop" through your opponent's files. It lacks the inquisitiveness of Interrogatories and the flexibility of depositions. Perhaps it's even wrong to call it a "discovery" tool since it comes into its own after discovery and is designed to summarize in a relatively concise form those facts which you already know and which are sufficiently definite that your opponent will admit them. Which leads to another point:

Don't Ask Two Questions in One.

Asking two questions in one leads to confusion and confusion leads to evasion and avoidance. For example, suppose you were to state: "The defendant was coming from a bank and was on his way to a department store."

The first part of this statement might well be true and the second part false. Don't expect your opposing counsel to do your work for you in separating the wheat from the chaff in your statements of fact. Keep them short, direct and simple. One fact per statement.

Don't Use Long, Convoluted Statements.

"On June 16, 1981, the Plaintiff withdrew $2,000.00 from Account 1234 at Jones Bank, rolled this over into a Certificate of Deposit at Smith Street Bank, deposited a small balance, and then went home."

You're wasting your time if Plaintiff left the bank and headed for the nearest bar! You're also wasting your time if he bought a Treasury Bill and not a Certificate, or if he challenges your idiosyncratic phrase, "rolled this over."

Don't Waste Your Time with Statements Concerning Opinion or Judgment.

"The Defendant knew that, in removing a prostate gland, using the supra-pubic technique is better than utilizing a trans-urethral resection."

That statement is not the proper realm of Requests for Admissions. It is judgmental in nature, and calls into question all manner of facts and opinions relating to the condition of the patient at the time a decision was made as to "how" to perform the necessary prostate operation. If you want to establish that a medical doctor negligently used a specific surgical technique and should have used a different one, you must go to depositions wherein you have the opportunity to engage in a vigorous dialogue with the doctor.

You should try to limit your statements to ones of fact. The whole idea is to try to get the opposition to admit as many facts as possible so that a Judge, on proper motion, can give you your judgment after he draws appropriate inferences and applies the applicable law.

Your opposing counsel will simply not let his client be boxed in by admitting an opinion statement. He or she will either deny the statement, object to it, or answer in such a manner that the response is valueless to you.

Since you know that this will happen, there is simply no point in spending time drafting statements concerning opinion matters that you know will not be admitted.

If it is necessary, you can sometimes skirt around matters of judgment by phrasing a question as a fact, thus:

> In Pittsburgh, Pennsylvania, during the year 1980, the technique most used by urologists for the removal of the prostate gland was a transurethral resection.

Now that statement may well be admitted if it is statistically correct and the fact is pretty well known in urological circles. The admission of such a fact may well help you by preparing the way for a series of questions you might want to ask in Interrogatories or at Depositions, but there isn't too much more that you can develop by means of Requests for Admissions.

Remember—try to stick to facts; leave opinions as a subject matter for other discovery techniques.

A REMINDER OF PRINCIPAL POINTS TO CONSIDER IN USING REQUESTS FOR ADMISSIONS

1. Try to win your case by using Requests in combination with a Motion for Summary Judgment.

   a) Always be conscious of the possibility of doing this.

   b) Analyze your case: do you already know most of the facts and is it likely you can force your opponent to admit them?

   c) Think of this in cases that depend on documentary evidence, statistics, or facts known by independent, third parties.

   d) Consider it as most likely in Assumpsit cases, land condemnation cases or disputes over title, Decedents Estate matters, or a Support case.

   e) Use it in a Trespass case where the disputed facts are few or where they can be established by "outside" witnesses.

2. Where you have many documents to use at trial use Requests for Admissions to establish authenticity, identity, and possibly to get them admitted as evidence.

3. Put your mind at ease by using Requests for Admissions to prove that inevitable group of "necessary nuisance" facts.

4. Do not ask two questions in one; stick to one fact per statement.

5. Avoid long, convoluted, complex statements.

6. Do not waste time with statements asking for opinions or judgments.

DO USE THIS DISCOVERY TOOL OFTEN!

Chapter 7

The Forceful Use of Motions in Aid of Discovery

When you become involved with discovery you might just as well be thoroughly acquainted with motion practice. The two go together like the proverbial love and marriage. I think I am safe in stating that there has *never* been extensive discovery in which one side or the other did not go running into Court with a motion for something or other. The litany of Motions is long: Motion to Compel Answers to Interrogatories, Motion for More Specific Answers to Interrogatories, Motion for Sanctions, Motion for Protective Order, Motion for Counsel Fees and Expenses and ultimately, hopefully, a Motion for Summary Judgment.

Why all the Motions? Because people won't do what you want them to do the way you want them to do it. They are obstreperous. This person refuses to produce a document, that one evades an Interrogatory, another refused to show up for a deposition, and a fourth shows up but won't answer certain questions. Most of the time the fault lies with a recalcitrant client, although sometimes opposing counsel is the culprit. The problems themselves are of a common, garden variety sort and the law provides these motions as a means for you to compel compliance with the rules.

Frequently there is a reasonable basis for a dispute. If you answer an important interrogatory the best you can, but not in the manner in which opposing counsel thinks you can and should, there could well be justification for an argument on the matter. A Motion to Compel Answers to Interrogatories is a good way to resolve the dispute. Perhaps you have been evasive in a matter in which you should have had a more direct answer.

When it comes to taking depositions or producing documents, there is frequently a broad area for legitimate disagreement. Many times in a deposition I have believed that the other attorney was taking advantage of the witness, or ranging far afield, and I have simply directed the witness not to answer the questions. If the other attorney wants them answered he or she can file a Motion and get a court order compelling the witness to answer. Of course my judgment (and yours) had better be pretty good because opposing counsel can also file a Motion for Counsel Fees and Expenses, and if the Court finds that my (or your) objection was frivolous or groundless we can end up with an Order directing that the witness appear and answer and, also, pay opposing counsel a fee and costs. That doesn't happen too often since one doesn't take such stern action with a witness unless one is on pretty solid ground.

EVASIVENESS AND REFUSAL TO COMPLY AS A TACTIC

You will find that some attorneys deliberately will avoid and evade your discovery procedures simply as a tactical maneuver to keep information from you. They figure that they have "two bites at the apple": (1) that it will be too much trouble for you to prepare a Motion, write a brief, and argue the matter in Court, and (2) they just might win the argument. To a certain degree they're right, and the tactic is a successful one. I find that large law firms adopt this tactic very often—and the basis for it is pure greed. It gives them an opportunity to bill a corporate client for an extensive brief (far out of proportion to the issues), and for an Argument. If they lose the argument they have really lost nothing for now they give you answers (or the documents) that you should have had all along. In the meantime, by a succession of these ploys they build up a substantial fee.

I'm always surprised that corporate clients put up with this sort of thing, but I take it that either they don't check the billings or the matter is justified somehow or other. Certainly it does not happen often where an individual or an insurance company is paying the bills. The individual can't bear the expense and the insurance company is too canny to put up with this nonsense.

Some individual lawyers do view this as a legitimate stalling tactic and will utilize it. The whole object is to wear you down so that you abandon or limit your discovery. It can't succeed unless you permit it to succeed. If you will be persistent, not only will you get the information you are after but also you will begin to wear down the other lawyer. Finally if this tactic can be established as a part of a pattern—occurring in relation to Interrogatories, Depositions and Production of Documents—it might reach the point where you can legitimately demand counsel fees and expenses for having to coerce the other side into giving you what you should have had under your Civil Rules.

The whole subject represents the "nasty" practice of law, is thoroughly unjustified, but is practiced often enough that you should be aware of it when it happens. You can't give in to this sort of thing just because it's the easy way to go.

BE PREPARED TO GO TO COURT OFTEN

Since most of the objections you will run into will have a legitimate basis (in the mind of adversary counsel), you must be prepared to go to Court—often. There can be no fooling around with this. You need the information—the other side has it—and you cannot let an objection stand in your way of securing the data. Since "open disclosure" is the established policy of our Judicial System, in this day, the inclination of any judge will be to require that the discovery be granted unless there is some exceptional reason why it should not. The burden is always on the shoulders of the person who objects to the discovery. You know that the rule is that you can secure not only all information that is relevant and germane to the lawsuit but also all other information that *can lead to* facts that are relevant to a lawsuit. When a judge begins to ponder the implications of that latter phrase he almost necessarily has to grant you your discovery, unless you have completely gone off the deep end. There are very few pertinent questions you can ask that cannot be interpreted as "leading to facts relevant to the lawsuit."

WATCH FOR BLANKET OBJECTIONS APPLIED TO A DOCUMENT, OR WRITING, PART OF WHICH IS RELEVANT

It will happen from time to time that a document will contain information that is helpful to you but will also have other information that is not relevant and that may be private, embarrassing, or very important to the other party. A letter, for example, might contain a valuable admission along with a personal love note. The attorney will object to showing you the letter. An income tax return may show itemized deductions that are relevant to your case but also show that the taxpayer earns part of his money by gambling—and an objection will be made.

These objections may be valid but they are no excuse for refusing to let you see the document—at least the part of it that is relevant. If you get along well with opposing counsel you can work out an agreement whereby he can cover up the personal or sensitive part of the document, make a copy, and give you the paper with only the pertinent sections showing. The same kind of agreement can be worked out with the tax return.

However, if you have any doubts go to court, demand the document, and insist that the judge review it to see whether the objectional material is as bad as it is supposed to be—and as irrelevant—or whether the objection is just a put-on.

You'll run into this from time to time: a psychiatric record reveals personal material that is not germane to the issues, love notes in a business letter, trade secrets mentioned in a report about the financial condition of a company, or income figures mentioned, as an aside, in an engineering report. You are still entitled to the document; the objectionable items can simply be blocked out and removed.

Let us look at some standard motions related to, and following, discovery:

I. MOTION TO COMPEL ANSWERS TO INTERROGATORIES, PRODUCTION OF DOCUMENTS, ATTENDANCE AT DEPOSITION, OR ANSWERS TO REQUESTS FOR ADMISSION

This is certainly the most common Motion you will be filing. It's unfortunate that we cannot devise a form you could keep in your form file, but the varieties of circumstances in which you will use this Motion are such that it is impractical. You simply have to prepare a separate, unique motion tailored to the particular facts with which you are confronted.

The motion itself should simply identify the particular discovery technique that was involved, state that the other side has failed to comply with the Rules in some particular manner or other, and ask the Court to compel the appropriate response.

As mentioned before, it is best to be able to state in the motion that you have orally endeavored to get the other side to cooperate, without success, and any letters you have sent asking for compliance with the Rules should be attached as Exhibits.

A note of caution or warning should be made at this time: you should not file a Motion like this until you have given opposing counsel a reasonable opportunity to respond to your discovery. If Answers to Interrogatories are due on May 20, I would not want to see a Motion to Compel Answers filed on May 21. The other attorney may have a good reason for the delay (he or she usually does), and it is to no one's advantage for you to rush in with a Motion. Instead, write a letter, or make a phone call, and try to solicit the discovery within a reasonable time. If, after an extension, courteously granted, there is still no reply, then file your Motion. You will have done all that can be expected of you.

If your complaint is that the other party has not fully or completely answered your Interrogatories or that the responses to Requests for Admissions have been evasive, then, in your motion, you should set forth the Interrogatory and the answer given (or Request and answer). That way the Court does not have to go through the pleadings to find your

Interrogatories and then go through the Interrogatories to find the ones you deem to be improperly answered. Thus:

> The Defendant has failed to answer, in full, Interrogatory No. 23 which reads:
>
> 23. Set forth the quantities of coal shipped by the Defendant on July 18, 1981 to:
>   a) Plaintiff's plant in Pittsburgh, Pennsylvania;
>   b) Plaintiff's plant in Des Moines, Iowa.
>
> ANSWER: 84,000 tons shipped.

Or, if the response is evasive:

> The Plaintiff has not properly answered Interrogatory No. 5. The Interrogatory, and Answer are:
>
> 5. State whether Plaintiff was driving the vehicle involved in this accident?
>
> ANSWER: Plaintiff was in the car.

In short, put the question and the response about which you are complaining up front where the Court can see it and get to it.

The following represents a typical Motion to Compel Answers to Interrogatories, which may also be used, with minor modifications, as a motion relating to the answers to Requests for Admission, or Production of Documents:

IN THE COMMON PLEAS COURT
OF ALLEGHENY COUNTY, PENNSYLVANIA

George Armstrong Custer	)	
Plaintiff,	)	
v.	)	No. 12345
Sitting Bull, Gall, and	)	*In Trespass*
Crazy Horse, Chiefs of	)	
the Sioux Indian Tribe,	)	
Defendants.	)	

MOTION TO COMPEL
ANSWERS TO INTERROGATORIES

NOW COME the Defendants by their attorney George Crook, Esquire, and do hereby move your Honorable Court as follows:

1. Interrogatories 1-22 were served upon counsel for Plaintiff on September 10, 1981.

2. Answers to the Interrogatories were filed on September 29, 1981.

3. Three of the Interrogatories were answered in an evasive manner, to wit:

a) Interrogatory No. 4:

Did you receive explicit warning from your scouts, while at the Crows Nest, on the morning of June 26, that a large camp of the Defendants was seen along the Little Big Horn River?

ANSWER: My eyes are good and I looked for myself.

b) Interrogatory No. 6:

Did you have specific instructions from General Terry to engage the Defendants on June 26?

ANSWER: General Terry trusted in my judgment in the matter.

(c) Interrogatory No. 7:

Did you make any specific effort to ascertain the numbers of Defendant's fellow citizens encamped along the Little Big Horn River before you ordered Major Reno to charge the Defendants on June 26?

ANSWER: I was confident that my instructions to Major Reno were correct.

None of the answers is responsive to the questions asked.

4. Two of the Interrogatories are not answered completely and fully:

a) Interrogatory No. 9 states:

Did you at any time on June 26 send troops down to the Little Big Horn River from

(1) Weir Point?
(2) Massacre Hill?

If the answer to each of the foregoing is "no," set forth in detail, by compass direction and distances, your exact course from Weir Point.

ANSWER: No.

b) Interrogatory No. 15:

On the afternoon of June 26, when you sent the companies of Capt. Keogh and Capt. Calhoun in a south-easterly direction along Battle Ridge,

(1) Were you attempting to contact Major Reno and/or Captain Benteen?
(2) What instructions did you give to each Captain named above?

ANSWER: Yes.

Counsel for Defendants requires full and complete answers to the Interrogatories before he can engage in additional discovery by way of either depositions or additional interrogatories.

WHEREFORE Your Honorable Court is respectfully requested to

enter an Order directing Plaintiff to answer in full, completely and directly, Interrogatories No's. 4, 6, 7, 9, and 15.

Respectfully Submitted,

_____

George Crook, Esquire
Attorney for Defendants

This kind of motion will get action from the Court and your discovery will proceed right on course.

II. MOTION FOR A PROTECTIVE ORDER

Sometimes your distinguished adversary counsel is going to do things, or ask for things, that just make you angry. He or she is simply going to go too far—either in scheduling depositions at a difficult time or place, or in serving voluminous Interrogatories (some of which are prying into personal matters and many of which have nothing to do with the case), or in demanding a document that he or she has no right to see. When you want to stop this misuse of discovery, file a Motion for a Protective Order.

In these situations you have to do something; you can't simply ignore the Notice of Deposition or the Interrogatories. Courts generally don't like your taking the position that certain discovery is, per se, improper and that you're not going to comply with it! It is possible that you are wrong and that if the other side files a Motion for Sanctions it just might be granted—and that can cause unnecessary problems.

It's far better, where you think that some discovery request goes beyond reasonable bounds, for you to bring the matter to the attention of the Court by way of a Motion for a Protective Order. It need not be lengthy and it requires no extensive briefing—just a recitation of the facts; if things are as clear as you think they are the motion will probably be granted, or some accommodation made. At least you let the Court rule on the matter instead of taking things into your own hands.

Let me present an illustrative motion.

Here Plaintiff's counsel, in a medical malpractice case, gave to the defense attorney an authorization to secure three hospital records and on the very same day served a Notice of Deposition to depose the Defendant a week later. There was just no way that the defense attorney could secure the records, discuss them with other physicians and hospital personnel, go over them with his client, and be prepared for a deposition in seven days. The defense attorney could simply have refused to appear on the day set for the deposition but that would have been an arbitrary way to handle the problem. He adopted the best course by filing this motion:

IN THE COURT OF COMMON PLEAS
OF ALLEGHENY COUNTY, PENNSYLVANIA

Frank Carlton)	
Plaintiff,)	
v.)	No: 6789
Andrew Hays M.D. and)	
City Hospital, a)	
Corporation,)	
Defendants.)	

MOTION FOR PROTECTIVE ORDER

AND NOW comes counsel for Andrew Hays, M.D. and moves the Court to enter a Protective Order with regard to the deposition proposed to be taken on July 8, 1981 at 10:30 A.M., notice having been served on or about July 1, 1981.

1. Counsel for the Defendant, Andrew Hays, M.D. moves that the Court order that the deposition of Andrew Hays, M.D. be taken after counsel for the defendant secures copies of all hospital records for the following reasons:

(a) Plaintiff's counsel only provided authorizations to secure all three hospital records with his letter of July 1, 1981.

(b) Counsel for the Defendant is attempting to secure the hospital records as quickly as possible.

(c) After securing the hospital records, counsel wishes to discuss the case and the hospital records with other medical personnel who were involved in the treatment of the Plaintiff.

(d) Counsel then wishes to discuss this case with his client so that Dr. Hays will be properly advised prior to his deposition.

(e) Counsel for Andrew Hays, M.D. does not believe that there are any circumstances which compel the taking of the deposition before he has been able to accomplish the foregoing.

(f) Counsel believes that he can secure the records and complete his investigations by August 1, 1981.

WHEREFORE, counsel for Andrew Hays, M.D. moves your Honorable Court to enter an Order postponing the deposition scheduled for July 8, 1981, to a date after August 1, 1981, to be selected by the Court.

_____

John E. Brown, Esquire
Attorney For Defendant

This is clear enough to enable a judge to see the problem and rule equitably.

There will be other situations of a similar nature that will occur periodically wherein you will want to curtail the other side's discovery or change the mechanics of it. Most of the time you can, and should, work this out with the other attorney, but when that becomes impossible file a Motion for a Protective Order and secure the help of the Court.

III. MOTION FOR SANCTIONS

This motion lies somewhere between a Motion to Compel (Answers to Interrogatories or Production of Documents, etc.) and a Motion for a Default Judgment, and might be considered an alternative to either of those motions. Let's assume that you have served Interrogatories on June 1. They are not answered by July 1 so you call opposing counsel and ask that the Answers be filed. In ten days or so there is no positive response, so you write a letter—to no avail. At this point it is best to file a Motion to Compel Answers to Interrogatories, reciting the facts, and securing a Court Order directing that the Answers be filed within a certain time. If that Order is not complied with, you have a decision to make—should you apply for a Judgment by Default or ask for some lesser penalty by way of a Motion for Sanctions?

I suspect that the answer to that puzzle lies in your analysis of your Court, the seriousness or significance of the discovery you are trying to secure, and your personal relations with the other attorney.

If your Court is of such a mind that it will not grant a Default Judgment, even for a violation of its own Order, then there is no purpose in going this route. We all know that there are judges like that. They are usually wonderful persons—kindhearted and sympathetic—who will simply refuse to take drastic action against a litigant or his (or her) attorney no matter how dilatory they may be. It has been my experience that this attitude varies with the size of the community, the number of lawyers at the Bar, the number of cases in litigation, and the pressure on the court to move cases and avoid delay. Thus a judge in a large metropolitan area, with a large caseload, will grant a Motion for a Default Judgment in exactly the same circumstances in which his, or her, brother in a small community will not. So be it.

A second criterion is the importance of the discovery. If all you have done is serve a half-dozen miscellaneous interrogatories, the Answers to which are really not very important, the chances are the Court will not exact a severe penalty for failure to answer. In such event you had better settle for a Motion for Sanctions and forget the Default Judgment. On the other hand, if you have prepared a careful set of Requests for Admissions that go to the very heart of the case, and the other side refuses to answer for the simple reason that to do so, honestly, would be to ruin their position, then you can and should ask for a Default Judgment.

Finally, your judgment should consider the opposing attorney. If he or she is a decent person who has some sensible explanation for the delay, or who has a willful and obstinate client, then you might opt for the Motion for Sanctions as a spur to the client, primarily. I have seen occasions when the other attorney was actually grateful that I filed the Motion when he or she had an incorrigble client who simply would not listen to reason. By filing the motion I took the other attorney off the hook, so to speak, and he or she could tell the client that whatever happens is all the client's fault.

If opposing counsel is one of those persons who have been habitually uncooperative and miserable to deal with, and the current refusal to respond to discovery and a Court Order is but the latest example, then you might as well go for the Default Judgment. You have heard the expression, "Don't get mad, get even." Well, this is your chance to "get even."

Frankly, if it's a serious matter and you have done everything in your power to secure compliance with the Rules and the other attorney is simply "stonewalling" his or her necessary response, then there is no use fooling around; apply for a Default Judgment. If there is any indication that you will hurt the other attorney unnecessarily, then apply for Sanctions.

The following represents a typical Motion for Sanctions:

IN THE COURT OF COMMON PLEAS
OF ALLEGHENY COUNTY, PENNSYLVANIA

American Graphics Corporation, a Pennsylvania Corporation, Plaintiff,	))))
v.	) No. 12345
Pictorial Specialty Shops, Inc., a Pennsylvania Corporation, Defendant.	) In Assumpsit))

MOTION FOR SANCTIONS

NOW COMES the Defendant, above named, by its counsel, Robert Brown, Esquire, and does hereby respectfully submit as follows:

1. A Notice of Deposition, directed to Harold Smith, President of Plaintiff, was filed on November 5, 1981 and served on counsel for Plaintiff on that date.

2. The deposition was to have been taken on November 20, 1981.

3. Harold Smith failed to appear for the deposition. No application for a continuance was ever filed and no explanation was given.

4. A Petition to Compel Attendance at Deposition was filed on November 29, 1981 and an Order of Court was entered on December 5, 1981, directing Harold Smith to appear for a deposition on December 15, 1981.

5. Harold Smith did not appear for a deposition on December 15, 1981. No request for a postponement was made nor has any explanation been given.

6. The failure of Harold Smith, President of Plaintiff Corporation, to appear and give testimony severely interferes with the right of Defendant to secure information needed to defend the allegations of the Complaint.

WHEREFORE, Your Honorable Court is respectfully requested to impose appropriate sanctions on Plaintiff (or, here name the specific sanction you desire) including attorneys' fees for the attendance of this counsel, twice, at the time and place of the depositions and the preparation and presentation of this Motion, and also Order Harold Smith to appear for a deposition on January 20, 1982, under threat of a Default Judgment for failure to do so.

Respectfully Submitted,

Robert Brown, Esquire
Attorney For Defendant,
Pictorial Specialty
Shops, Inc.

When the Court signs an Order to this effect you will get compliance from the opposing party in nearly every case. It is rare to find someone who will ignore this Order, but occasionally it will happen.

At the Argument, you will have to rely on the practice in your jurisdiction in deciding whether to suggest specific sanctions or leave that matter to the Court. In either event, with a Motion like this, you are going to get some action.

IV. MOTION FOR DEFAULT JUDGMENT

A Motion for Default Judgment has all the influence of a .357 Magnum in catching, and holding, the attention of opposing counsel. It commands *respect*. Your opponent knows that he had done something that you think is seriously wrong when you are driven to the point of filing this motion.

A Motion for Default is of the "last gasp" variety and should never be filed frivolously. In order for a Court to consider it seriously, and to be willing to grant it, you must have filed earlier Motions to compel compliance with your discovery efforts, secured an Order of Court directing same, be able to show efforts on your part to get the opposition to respond—and to show a complete failure of all of these endeavors. Remember that Courts do not like to decide cases on the basis of pleadings or attorney dilatoriness. They would rather permit the Pleadings to be amended and discipline the lazy attorney. That is why so many Motions for Judgment on the Pleadings, for Summary Judgment, and for Default are usually denied. If an issue of fact can be found, a Motion for Summary Judgment will be denied; if the law is the least bit ambiguous or uncertain, or the Pleadings can be amended, a Motion for Judgment on the Pleadings will be denied; and if the Court can find some excuse for the conduct of your opposing party or its counsel, your Motion for a Default Judgment will be denied.

It isn't often that you can use this legal weapon, but when you can the effects are devastating. The case ends very abruptly. There are two important prerequisites to using this Motion.

1. Always have a Court Order in existence which has not been complied with.

Any judge will want you to have made some effort to secure compliance with the Rules by gentler means. Thus, you will have to have filed a Motion to Compel Answers to Interrogatories, or to Produce Documents, or Answers to Requests for Admissions, and secured an Order of Court. That Order should state that counsel has a definite time period (30 days, for example, or "until April 21") to comply and, preferably, should contain the express words "or suffer a default," "or a default judgment will be entered." Thus both the time limitation and the threat will be clear and definite.

2. Always be prepared to show your good faith effort to secure compliance.

After opposing counsel has allowed the time limit to expire, write one or two letters asking for compliance with the court order and make one or two telephone calls. If you don't, the average judge will be inclined to give the negligent attorney "one more time." His or her mood will change if you can prove that you already gave counsel his "one more chance" and that there is no need or purpose for additional leniency. The average judge will buy that. So, with those two escapes effectively blocked, your motion stands an excellent chance of being granted.

One more thing—if opposing counsel does not have a strong explanation to justify his or her defiances of a Court Order and your letters, the filing of this Motion will probably bring a quick request for settlement negotiations, and you're going to be in an excellent position to get the highest reasonable figure for your case. Do not use this opportunity foolishly by trying to push the other attorney into a corner and asking for the "sun, moon and stars" in settlement—that will simply provoke a fight and you may end up with no settlement and no chance to get that figure in a verdict. Instead, stick with your "highest reasonable demand" and you have a good chance of getting it.

A good example of a Motion for Default Judgment is the following:

IN THE COURT OF COMMON PLEAS
OF ALLEGHENY COUNTY, PENNSYLVANIA

Lucy Jones and Henry Jones, her husband, Plaintiffs,	)))
v.	) No. 12345
Brown Pharmaceutical Company., Inc., a Corporation. Defendant.	))))

MOTION FOR DEFAULT JUDGMENT AS TO BROWN PHARMACEUTICAL CO., INC.

Now come Plaintiffs above named by their Attorney James B. Black, Esquire, and do hereby respectfully move for a Default Judgment for the following reasons:

1. This Honorable Court entered an Order on July 12, 1981, directing this Defendant to answer Interrogatories within 30 days or suffer a default judgment.

2. It is now 60 days later and Defendant refuses to answer the interrogatories.

3. The Interrogatories were originally served on April 21, 1981, some 5½ months ago.

4. Counsel for Plaintiff requested the Answers in letters dated August 19 and September 15, 1981, copies of which are attached hereto and marked as Exhibits 1 and 2. Defendant kept promising Answers but they were never sent. See letters of August 29, and September 21, 1981, marked Exhibits 3 and 4.

5. Plaintiff has taken every conceivable action to be cooperative. An Order of Court was secured, letters have been written, and phone calls have been made.

6. Discovery has simply come to a halt for 5½ months, as to this Defendant.

7. Plaintiff has been seriously jeopardized in terms of securing informa-

tion from Defendant, in having data from which to decide who should be deposed, and in deciding whether additional, supplemental interrogatories should be prepared and served.

8. It is now 3½ months since the Order of this Court.

9. This case represents a flagrant disregard of the Order of this Court and the Rules of Civil Procedure.

WHEREFORE, your Honorable Court is respectfully requested to enter a Default Judgment as to Brown Pharmaceutical Co., Inc.

Respectfully Submitted,

_____

James B. Black
Attorney for Plaintiffs

Another example, somewhat along the same line, is this Motion:

IN THE COURT OF COMMON PLEAS
OF ALLEGHENY COUNTY, PENNSYLVANIA

Thomas W. Green and	)
Rose M. Green, his wife	)
Plaintiffs,	)
v.	) No. 26809
William C. Smith, M.D.,	)
and City Hospital, a	)
Corporation,	)
Defendants.	)

MOTION FOR DEFAULT JUDGMENT AS TO WILLIAM C. SMITH, M.D.

Now come the Plaintiffs, above named, by their attorney, John Brown, Esquire, and do hereby respectfully submit as follows:

1. On October 11, 1981, Interrogatories 1-20 were served on Defendant, William C. Smith, M.D.

2. The Answers were due on November 11, 1981.

3. Defendant has been requested, both by letter and by telephone, to answer the Interrogatories. See Exhibit 1 attached hereto.

4. A Motion to Compel Answers to Interrogatories was filed and served on December 30, 1981.

5. On January 9, 1982, the Court entered an Order directing that the Answers be filed by January 29, 1982.

6. It is now ten days beyond the deadline established by the Court—and nearly four months since the Interrogatories were served—and no Answers have been filed.

7. The failure of this Defendant to respond to the Order of Court, and Rules of Civil Procedure, evidences a studied contempt for, and reckless disregard of, his responsibilities in this lawsuit and has caused serious harm to the Plaintiffs. The Plaintiffs have clearly been disadvantaged in the preparation and development of their case by the willful conduct of the Defendant.

WHEREFORE, your Honorable Court is respectfully requested to enter a Default Judgment in favor of Plaintiffs and against Defendant, William C. Smith, M.D.

_____

John Brown
Attorney For Plaintiffs

These Motions are extremely effective. You can rest assured that one of three things will happen:

1. The Court will grant your motion and you will get a judgment;
2. The opposing party will be pushed into a prompt discussion of settlement;
3. You will get the discovery that initiated the whole affair.

One thing you will not get is additional procrastination from the other side—and that you can do without.

V. MOTION FOR SUMMARY JUDGMENT

Certainly this motion has to be the culmination of well-prepared, effective discovery.

By the nature of things it isn't often that you will be able to use this device. You will recall the legal maxim that a Summary Judgment cannot be granted if there is any question of fact relating to the ultimate issue in the case. If there is an issue of fact the case must be tried—whether to a jury or a judge.

Nonetheless from time to time you do elicit every significant fact from your opponent in such manner that a Motion for Summary Judgment is appropriate and can succeed.

It is necessary, when you file your motion, that it be supported by facts that are admitted under oath or affidavit. The Court will not consider matters that are not under oath nor, of course, anything de hors the record. Answers to Interrogatories and Answers to Requests for Admissions will, of necessity, be a part of the pleadings but many times attorneys do not file transcripts of depositions. You will have to make certain that they are filed if you intend to make reference to them in your motion. In addition, if you have secured documents from the other side pursuant to a Request (or Motion) for Production, keep in mind that you must have these verified somehow or other—either in a deposition or by use of Requests for Admissions. Even though you secured them from the opposition they cannot, per se, be used to support a Summary Judgment. Their authenticity must be established under oath.

ATTACH IMPORTANT EXTRACTS FROM THE RECORD IN YOUR MOTION

In the Motion itself you will make reference to the location of the specific facts that support the motion, i.e., "See Answer to Interrogatory No. 12, Request for Admission No's. 3, 4, 6, 9, and 10; Deposition of Mary Smith, P. 12," but you should also include a reasonable amount of this material in the body of the motion. This has two salutary effects: (1) it heightens and dramatizes the importance of the material you have selected, and (2) it saves the Court the necessity of searching through the pleadings to find the important admissions you refer to and acts as a summary of the more important ones.

To illustrate, let's take the case of a person who agrees to become a co-owner with an aged relative of a bank account so that he can physically do the banking for his uncle and also pay some of the routine bills. The lawsuit exists, of course, because the other party begins to help himself to the funds and transfers them to a Certificate of Deposit in his name alone. Now, at a deposition you effectively get the other party to agree (1) that no money of his went into the account; (2) that the money was to be used solely for the purposes of the senior citizen; (3) that this money was used to buy the Certificate of Deposit, and (4) that, in reality, it belongs to the aged relative.

Now the deposition itself may be 50 pages long, tracing the origins of the account and deposits into and withdrawals from the account. In your motion you can make such references to the deposition as you deem necessary (referring to pages), but when you come to the really vital admissions, be sure to do one of two things:

1. Quote directly from the deposition, or,

2. Attach that page of the deposition as an Exhibit to the Motion.

This is the Motion that was filed:

John Jones,	)
Plaintiff,	) Civil Division
v.	)
Frank Smith,	) No: 1234
Defendant.	)

MOTION FOR SUMMARY JUDGMENT

Now comes the Plaintiff, above named by his attorney, James Black, Esquire, and does hereby respectfully submit as follows:

1. The Plaintiff and Defendant are Uncle and Nephew in relationship. (Deposition of Frank Smith P. 3.)

2. This action is one to recover funds given by the Plaintiff to Defendant as a matter of convenience to be used solely for the purposes of the needs of Plaintiff and at the direction of Plaintiff. (Deposition of Frank Smith P. 4.)

3. Plaintiff alleges that the funds were fraudulently and improperly transferred to Certificates of Deposit and a savings account in the name of Defendant alone and that Defendant refused to return said funds to Plaintiff. (See paragraphs 5 and 6 of Complaint.)

4. In a deposition taken on August 19, 1981, in this matter, Defendant has admitted that:

a) all of the moneys in certificates of deposit ($20,000.00) in his name and in a savings account ($3,164.44) in his name, belong solely to the Plaintiff.

b) no portion of said moneys belongs to him (the Defendant).

c) he will return said moneys to the Plaintiff.

5. The following colloquy is from Pages 28 and 29 of the deposition of defendant, Frank Smith:

> Q All right. So that at the present time you have in your name two certificates of deposit; is that correct?
>
> A Yes, sir.
>
> Q And each is for $10,000.00?
>
> A Yes, sir.
>
> Q What is it—City Bank—and what is it—Area Savings Bank?
>
> A Yes, sir.
>
> Q You also have in the Savings Account at City Bank a balance— is it approximately $3,000.00?
>
> A Approximately.
>
> Q And it is still there; is it?
>
> A Yes, sir.
>
> Q And is it your understanding that this is money belonging to John Jones?
>
> A It is.
>
> Q And do you agree to turn over this money to him?
>
> A Yes, sir.

Q   And likewise, the balance that still remains in the City Bank
    Savings Account, will you turn that money over?

A   I will.

MR. BLACK: Okay. I think that is all I have.

6. There is no other issue of fact in this lawsuit.

WHEREFORE, Your Honorable Court is respectfully requested to
enter a Summary Judgment in favor of Plaintiff John Jones and against
Defendant Frank Smith in the sum of $23,164.44 together with costs of
this suit.

Respectfully Submitted,

_____

James Black
Attorney For Plaintiff

The little excerpt from the deposition does tend to catch one's
attention and is a nice little summary of the position counsel will adopt at
the Argument.

You will not want to go into too much detail in the motion—save the
lengthy references to the Record for your Brief—but just put in enough
material so that, upon reading the motion, the Court will see that you are
very serious about this and that you have a strong case.

If you will refer back to the discussion on page 131 you will there see
the effective use of a Motion for Summary Judgment based on the failure to
answer Requests for Admission. The Court accepted the Requests as true,
found that no issue of fact existed, and entered the Summary Judgment.

As I stated previously, it isn't often that you are going to have the basis
for a Motion for Summary Judgment, but it does occur from time to time
and you should always be ready to take advantage of these opportunities.

SEVEN KEYS TO THE MOST EFFECTIVE USE OF MOTIONS

1. The principal motions that you will use in aid of Discovery or
   following Discovery are:
   a) Motion to Compel (Answers to Interrogatories, Answers to
      Requests for Admissions, etc.)
   b) Motion for a Protective Order.
   c) Motion for Sanctions.
   d) Motion for Default Judgment.
   e) Motion for Summary Judgment.

2. Do not hesitate to file a motion when your discovery is unjustifiably
   delayed by the other side.

3. Do not take it upon yourself to refuse to comply with requested discovery; use a Motion for a Protective Order.

4. If discovery is continuously delayed, file a Motion for Sanctions. Ask for counsel fees and a date certain for performance of the desired response to your discovery.

5. Use a Motion for Default Judgment as a last resort. Before you use it have:

   a) A prior Order of Court directing response to your discovery by a certain date; and

   b) Letters to opposing counsel, asking for the discovery which you can use as an Exhibit.

6. File a Motion for Summary Judgment when it is clear that your discovery has resolved all issues of fact in your favor.

7. REMEMBER: Delay, evasion and avoidance can work only if you permit it to go unchallenged. FILE YOUR MOTIONS and keep the discovery process moving ahead.

Chapter 8

Settlement—Achieving the Goal

The *only* purpose in indulging in the various discovery procedures that have been discussed in this book is either to get your case in such condition that you can try it well, or to settle it on terms favorable to yourself. That is the pay-off. To be frank, the end result I much encourage is settlement, and good, thorough discovery should make every case "settleable." By the time you conclude discovery you should have a pretty clear idea of the nature of your case. If it is exceptionally strong, or weak, it is a prime candidate for settlement; if it falls within that broad middle range of cases about which you can say "I have a shot at winning it" (but with serious reservations), then discovery will have enabled you to know precisely where your strengths and weaknesses lie. These are the troublesome cases and they comprise the bulk of those that go to trial. They should—and can—be settled, but it does take (1) some *hard work* and (2) *lengthy bargaining*.

THE TRIALS AND TRIBULATIONS OF SETTLEMENT

No case is settled with one telephone call or one casual conversation. Would that they were! It takes time, energy and effort to bring about a settlement, and that is the principal reason why more cases are not settled in the hiatus between completion of discovery and trial. It's hard work, associated with an uncertain conclusion. Given that combination, it's not surprising that many lawyers prefer to postpone making hard decisions and instead wait until the day of trial when pressure forces hasty conferences, snap judgments, and a settlement for good or ill, quickly arrived at. This is all right—except for the fact that most of the time the case could have been settled six or more months earlier for the same figure, and many settlements made in this manner are poor ones. Someone gets burned.

It doesn't have to be that way. Granted that the settlement process can be laborious and frustrating. The careful efforts of both Plaintiff and Defense counsel can result in a conclusion long before trial—and one that is fair and reasonable.

Unfortunately the burden, in settlement negotiations, is relatively one-sided—the Plaintiff's attorney usually has the task of initiating the subject and keeping it moving. He or she is the one who wants some money, and the Defendant (whether individual, business corporation or insurance company) finds it painful to pay and tends to drag its feet to avoid doing so. Thus the Plaintiff's attorney finds himself or herself in the position of being the person who:

(1) Has to initiate the negotiations;

(2) Must make the telephone calls and the seemingly endless follow-up calls;

(3) Has to collect the tax returns, profit and loss statements, or bills and medical reports, and send them to the defendant;

(4) Must keep pressuring the local claims people to put pressure on that faceless, anonymous individual in the home office whose decision is holding up the settlement;

(5) Has to try to satisfy that person with more documentation—wage records, photographs, death certificates and other papers; and

(6) Must keep his or her client informed with what he or she is trying to accomplish.

This work cannot be done quickly because there are so many people involved. To begin with, one deals with opposing counsel who then confers with the client who then may consult with various specialists—accountants, experts in the field of work involved, committees of different kinds, and decision-making officers of a corporation. When a decision is made it comes back down through the chain to the Plaintiff's attorney and then to his client. If an offer is rejected and a new demand is made it goes back to the Defense attorney and he or she starts through the whole process again. Along the way, of course, someone asks for more data so that the process is short-circuited until the demand is satisfied and straightened out. This can happen several times.

Thus the delay.

Granted that the settlement process takes time and is hard work, the result justifies the effort. Anytime you can close a case, months before trial, with a settlement that satisfies you and your client, you can be assured that the effort was worthwhile.

SETTLEMENT VIS-À-VIS TRIAL

I am a Trial Lawyer. You are a Trial Lawyer. Yet if the truth be known, neither of us tries, to verdict, six cases a year. If you are a defense attorney you might get above that figure since defense attorneys usually try more cases than Plaintiff's lawyers. The reason for that is simple enough: the defense business is usually concentrated in a relatively small number of law firms while the Plaintiff's Bar is composed of a large number of individuals or small-member firms, all of whom have a few cases filed in Court at any one time.

If you doubt my statistics go to your Court Administrator and find the number of jury verdicts last year; you will be shocked at their small number. Even if you include Non-Jury cases, the total, in comparison with the number of cases filed, will be around ten to 15 percent or less.

I took the opportunity to check this recently in my own Court. Allegheny County, Pennsylvania, with 1,450,085 people, ranks as the twelfth most populous county in the United States and, as you would expect, has its fair share of litigation. Yet in reviewing the 1980 Annual Report for the Court of Common Pleas I learned that only 258 cases were tried to verdict! How many cases were settled at some stage in the judicial process? 1,876 cases. Of the total number of jury trial cases handled by our Civil Division, 2,134 cases, only 12 percent went to verdict. Obviously 88 percent settled. That is a matter for sober reflection. Since so many cases do settle, why not settle them promptly after you have completed discovery and when both you and opposing counsel know practically all that you are ever going to know about the case? It should be done and it can be done. The burden rests on you to initiate settlement discussions, to keep them moving, and to reach a satisfactory conclusion.

Let's face reality—settlement is the life blood of our judicial system. And it's an absolute necessity for the monetary success of many lawyers—especially the Plaintiff's lawyers who work on a contingent fee basis. When you think about trying every case, just remember two things:

1. It's a long wait between trials, and while you're waiting there is no money coming in; and

2. You have to lose some cases, and on those cases your fee is zero, which doesn't pay the rent or put food on the table.

On the defense side one might suggest that insurance companies and industrial corporations begin to complain as your hourly charges reach mountainous heights, and the complaints become an uproar if the conclusion is a high verdict which they have to pay. It's also quite embarrassing if the case wasn't worth much to begin with and your fee bill turns out to be higher than the verdict!

So it behooves all of us to take a long look at settlement as the proper basis for concluding a case—and all the results of your discovery should be utilized toward accomplishing a good settlement.

AFTER DISCOVERY, THE PRINCIPAL HANGUP TO SETTLEMENT IS YOU

Despite their years of training and experience and their professionalism, many lawyers still find it difficult to "look the facts in the face" and act on what they see. How very often I have heard a Plaintiff's attorney say, "It's not much of a case but I'm going to try it and see what happens." What "happens" 95 times out of a hundred is that he tries the case and loses it. Such persons are mesmerized with the gambling instinct, and view a trial much like the roll of the dice. They forget that nearly all gamblers are poor men. On the defense side one hears the flippant remark, "I don't have a very good case but Plaintiff wants too much money and maybe I can bring it in at a lower figure." This quite ignores the fact that if Plaintiff does have a good case, he or she is quite justified in making a demand somewhat higher than ordinary and a reasonable jury will probably agree with him or her. Yet the attorney just can't bring himself or herself to acknowledge that the demand is justified by the facts and ought to be paid.

It's hard to put a name on this attitude. Perhaps it's a combination of pride (arrogance), a little greed on Plaintiff's part, or a miserly, stingy attitude built into the defense attorney. Certainly stubbornness and vanity have a lot to do with it. Occasionally stupidity plays a role. Whatever the reason, the attitude and its end result are not professionalism. The very concept of "lawyering" demands a high degree of objectivity, honesty, good judgment and self-control. Venality and a whimsical attitude truly belong at a race track and not in a lawyer's office.

When you have carefully exhausted your discovery techniques and have all the facts available, it is time to say to yourself, "If I analyze this case carefully and properly there has to be a settlement here." Most of the time you'll be right.

WHEN SHOULD YOU BEGIN SETTLEMENT NEGOTIATIONS?

There are two aspects to every case—the liability side and damages. When you have established your case on the liability side as firmly as you can, it is time to begin to prepare for settlement negotiations. That is the major hurdle in nearly every case. When you have the answer to the question "Can we win?" then the issue of "How much do we pay?" almost naturally falls into place. Certainly one must inquire at great length into the question of losses or injury, but that is done to verify the claims and to narrow the range of potential payment. But the principal decision affecting settlement is the one involving the "Can we win?" question.

I caution you at once that it is a mistake to answer that crucial question with a simplistic "yes" or "no" answer. A quick overview of your file might lead to the impression, "I have a pretty good case here," and that may be true, but a detailed analysis is necessary before you can say "how good" is "pretty good." There are several facts to consider:

1. Can Plaintiff get past a non-suit?
2. How many witnesses can each side produce on the liability question?
3. How strong are these witnesses?
4. Can their testimony be buttressed by documentary evidence?
5. Do you have damaging admissions that can be presented in Court?
6. Is the Law definite and clear on the subject matter of this lawsuit, or is it in a state of flux?
7. Is the attorney—your opponent—skilled and careful or is he, or she, inexperienced, reckless, or lazy?
8. How have cases like this fared, in your court, in the past?
9. If this case is assigned to a Judge, or you have an idea which Judge may handle it, what do you expect his, or her position to be?

When one speaks of appraising a case for settlement, all these factors have to be considered and then you can answer the question, "How good is my case?" And you might find yourself answering—I can win this case...

- Unless Judge Smith hears it;
- If witness Jones hold up;
- Provided Sam Brown tries it and not a better lawyer in that firm;
- If the Appellate Court doesn't change the law on the case pending before them;
- If the other side does not bring in those witnesses who have moved to Florida.
- And so on—and on—and on.

You know, as I do, that all cases have problems, so let's not delude ourselves that we are positively going to try this particular case. Now that discovery is concluded, analyze your case carefully and make every effort to settle it NOW! This is no horse race, so put your gambling instincts aside and take a long careful look at the facts and your degree of proof.

SIX KEYS TO EFFECTIVE SETTLEMENTS

1. Settlements are not merely desirable; they are necessary to your financial well-being.
2. Begin to form your idea about settlement when the liability problem becomes clear.
3. Carefully consider *all* the elements that lead to success or failure—the facts, law, quality of witnesses, supporting evidence and the important "outside" factors.
4. Study your file seriously and in detail.
5. Put away the gambler instinct and be objective, disciplined and honest in your analysis.
6. Avoid delay; when Discovery is finished proceed at once to work on settlement.

Now, let's go to work on achieving a settlement:

I. START WITH A CLIENT CONFERENCE

If cases were left with the lawyers, I daresay that $99^{99}/_{100}$ percent would be settled. Unfortunately, lawsuits belong to the litigants, not to the lawyers. And clients often take an entirely different view of people, events and amounts than do their attorneys.

In this respect Defense attorneys are usually in a much better position than the Plaintiff's lawyer. Most defendants in this day and age are insurance companies and commercial businesses. The persons involved are often well educated and always experienced. A Claim Supervisor or Manager has been doing claim work for years. He knows the law, can appreciate the "weight of the evidence," is familiar with the "going rate" and possible exposure in a given type of case, and is constantly making value judgments. He has probably dealt with the same defense firm for years and has worked out a good relationship and modus operandi. He or she will respond easily to your reasoned and sensible analysis of the case.

The business executive is in much the same position. He, too, is called upon, almost daily, to analyze facts and figures and to make judgments in an impartial and objective manner. It's second nature to him. If the litigant is a corporation, it has a law department or a firm that provides legal advice and direction, and these people have no other purpose than to evaluate the facts, know the law, and, applying the one to the other, exercise a judgment as to the best course to follow. As a result they will listen attentively to your proposal and will be inclined to follow your advice.

The Plaintiff's attorney, on the other hand, has no such good fortune. While it is true that our Courts entertain many lawsuits between corporations, most of the plaintiff-litigants are individuals. The vast majority of these people are woefully ignorant of law, do not spend their days amassing and analyzing facts, and habitually do not make judgmental decisions. To make things worse, the ordinary plaintiff is the person who has been injured or, in an Assumpsit matter, suffered a grievous financial loss, so that there is a great deal of raw emotion involved in his or her every thought concerning the lawsuit.

Whichever type your client may be, the first step in effecting a settlement is to secure the consent and advice of the client.

1. Educate the Client.

One thing is certain in every case—the client has turned the case over to you, with trust and confidence in your abilities, and by that act has signified his or her willingness to be guided by your good judgment. So begin your efforts by working with the client. In doing so there are a few things you must prepare for:

2. Know Your Case Well.

You can't do a selling job if you don't know what you're talking about. You must have gone through your file thoroughly—beginning with the pleadings, extracting pertinent Answers to Interrogatories, flagging certain pages in the depositions, noting the answers to particular Requests for Admissions, and jotting down the impressions of your investigator after his interviews with witnesses. If you think it necessary prepare a little memo on the applicable law, especially if there has been a recent change or it is in a confused and uncertain state.

3. Have an Opinion and Express it.

Your job is to give advice. The client retained you as an expert and you are expected to express a strong, definite opinion concerning the proper course of action. A busy executive does not want to hear your analysis of the case followed by a plaintive query, "What do you want me to do, sir?" He'll tell you soon enough what he wants to do after you have told him what you think he ought to do and why.

In like manner your individual lay client doesn't know any more about analyzing a lawsuit than he does about flying a plane or performing an operation. That's why he hired you. He or she wants you to decide what is the best thing to do. Sometimes they don't like what they hear, but they understand that you know more about the subject than they do.

I find it aggravating to sit with another attorney, from time to time, while he explains the case in a vague, general manner, then offhandedly says, "Well, it's up to you—whatever you want to do." How in the world can he expect the client to make a sensible decision when the client lacks knowledge, experience and expertise? I have found that this is a common fault among attorneys who are not active in litigation matters. They lack confidence in their ability to justify their opinion and prefer not to express one at all! This is wrong and should be absolutely avoided.

HAVE A DEFINITE OPINION, EXPRESS IT WITH
VIGOR, AND BE PREPARED TO JUSTIFY IT!

4. Talk About a Range of Settlement, Not a Particular Figure.

When you discuss settlement, the bottom line is money. Defendants ask, "How much shall we pay?" Plaintiffs ask, "What can we get"?

Under no circumstances should you permit yourself to be boxed in by agreeing on a specific sum. It's a mistake to say, "This case should be settled for $12,500.00," or any other precise figure. To begin with, at this stage you don't know if you can get that figure, and, second, the amount itself becomes a fixation in the mind of the client. If you do this as a Plaintiff's attorney and the final offer is $11,750.00 the client may well reject it on the ground that "you told us it was worth $12,500.00." If you're a Defense attorney and by hard bargaining you drive the Plaintiff down to $13,500.00, you may find yourself the butt of some snide comments from the home office about your evaluation. As I mentioned before, the experience of the Claim Supervisor, together with your explanation, may well result in your getting the extra $1,000.00, but the Plaintiff's attorney— dealing with an emotional and inexperienced client—will hear that wail of "You told me $12,500.00" for the duration of the case.

From a practical point of view it's better to talk to your client in terms of a settlement range. If you can convince a client that the case should be settled if you can negotiate a figure "between $15,000.00 and $20,000.00," you're in a much better position. It gives you some needed flexibility and the client does not become unalterably attached to a specific sum of money.

5. Get the Client Committed—in Writing.

Once you have discussed the case with your client and have batted around various monetary values, come to some final conclusion about a settlement range. Don't let the client leave the office with the matter just hanging in the air. You should beware of phrases like "See what you can do," "Talk to the other side and get back to me," "Get a firm offer (or demand) and I'll let you know." Those comments are anathema. Why? Because they're meaningless. When you finally negotiate with the other side that person wants you to have (1) a reasonable degree of authority, and (2) a figure, or figures, in mind that can be the basis for firm negotiation. Otherwise your adversary is dealing with ephemera—nonsense talk. Why waste the time?

As to the suggestion that the agreement with the client be in writing, this, for defense attorneys, will be a matter of routine correspondence.

With Plaintiff's attorneys it's a different matter. Many Plaintiff's attorneys do not do this and I know that it is a constant source of irritation, confusion, and ill-feelings. The common cause is simply slipshod office administration combined with a pious hope that it's not necessary. It's also a mistake. Given the ability of many clients to "disremember" what was discussed at your conference regarding evaluation, and considering the natural desire of most clients to have second thoughts and want "more" and then to claim confusion and misunderstanding when you remind them of the agreed-upon settlement range—granted all of that, do yourself a favor and GET IT IN WRITING. All it takes is a simple memo that you can prepare in a few moments:

MEMO OF AGREEMENT REGARDING SETTLEMENT

October 10, 1981.

I, James Jones, do hereby acknowledge that I have discussed my case against Smith Company with my attorney on this date. We have reviewed all aspects of the case, its merits and problems have been explained to me, and my attorney has given me his evaluation of the case. I agree that if the defendant makes any offer in the range of $15,000.00 to $20,000.00, I will accept it and I authorize my attorney to negotiate on that basis.

_____

James Jones, Plaintiff

Witness:

_____

_____

It's always advisable to have someone witness the Agreement, even if it is the wife, a friend, or your secretary. It's amazing how a person who wants to forget a commitment will finally acknowledge that he made it if prodded by a child, spouse, friend, or third party.

You should run off twenty or so of these forms and keep them in your form file for the occasions when you need them. This practice is extremely beneficial, because there is nothing more embarrassing than to negotiate a settlement and then have to go back to your opposing attorney and tell him or her that the deal is off and that you need more money, or that you can't pay the amount you agreed on. This creates antagonism, gives the appearance that you don't know what you're doing, and damages your credibility. Protect yourself; have the memo signed—and nearly always your client will abide by it.

REMEMBER THESE RULES

1. Educate your client.
2. Know your case thoroughly.
3. Have a definite opinion and express it.
4. Discuss a range and not a precise amount.
5. Get your client committed in writing.

II. NEGOTIATE THE SETTLEMENT

Dealing with the client is just plain hard work; negotiating the settlement is fun. All parties have an understanding of the law, the facts, and some of the intangibles that go into settlement negotiations. (Is so-and-so a good witness? Are we a target defendant? Is the law about to be changed? In what county or district will the case have to be tried?) In short, everyone knows the rules of the game.

This is the time to pull together your data, polish up your powers of persuasion, and make your discovery pay off.

The first thing to do is to gather every salient fact, restricting yourself to crucial, significant matters. (Settlement negotiations are not like trying a case in court where you have to be prepared to prove every fact.) All the other side is really interested in is whether you can genuinely prove the gravaman of your case. So stick to that. Pull out the admissions in the depositions, the peripheral support in the Answers to Interrogatories, the significant documents, and the damning Answers to Requests for Admissions.

Now call your opponent and set up a meeting. (Do not negotiate on the telephone unless you really know the opposing attorney very well, have dealt with him for a long time, and the two of you understand each other thoroughly. Otherwise the conversation becomes just another telephone call with little significance and poor results.) When you arrive be prepared to overwhelm him or her with the solid case you have developed. Unless you have deceived yourself the time will come when he or she has to acknowledge that you have a winner. But before this happens there will be much justifying and shifting ground. That is why you must have anticipated some counter-argument and prepared the data to meet it. It's impressive as can be when your opponent tries to shift the blame in some manner and you can produce a document that shows that "it just ain't so," or he tries to claim that his client misunderstood a portion of a contract and you can point to the deposition of a partner which shows that he understood very well indeed. It's this kind of thing that leads to good settlements. As long as your opposing attorney can rely on "imaginative talk" and bluff, you're not going to get anywhere. When you can meet his or her arguments with facts and documents, sooner or later it becomes obvious that you are in a pretty good condition.

Even Questionable Cases Can Be Settled.

If, after you review the product of all of your discovery, you realize that yours is not the greatest case in the world, even then do not hesitate to approach opposing counsel about settlement. Most cases are in this category—in which each side has something to say about the event at issue but neither is in an especially strong position.

Thanks to discovery you can now see the flaws in your case very clearly. If you will evaluate the case with those flaws in mind you have a good chance of settling it. Above all—don't succumb to the temptation to hold it for trial when you know in advance that it's a weak case. That leads to a terrible waste of time, money and effort. Aging is good for wine, not for weak cases.

Instead, once again, go to opposing counsel prepared to point out—vigorously—the many problems that he or she has, while acknowledging your own. I find that humor, candor, and a realistic appraisal of the case will work wonders. When the case is laid out for both you and your opponent to see clearly, with the gaps and missing links shining like the stars at night, then, most surely, a common agreement and understanding can be reached. Neither attorney wants to try a case when the proofs, as to each of them, remind one of Swiss cheese, and the only argument is whose slice has the biggest holes!

III. ARRIVE AT THE SETTLEMENT RANGE

There is no working area in the law that is more difficult than this—how to arrive at the proper figure for settlement. Pulling figures out of the clear blue sky doesn't work; they are always unrealistic. There is not—yet—any computer to solve the problem. At least, in most Assumpsit cases, the facts themselves set the outer limits of recovery, but that's not true of Trespass cases, with the sole exception perhaps of a Wrongful Death case where the death was instantaneous. How does one evaluate a Sexual Harassment case or a claim for damages for a violation of Civil Rights? In any case in which intangibles are involved—pain, loss of opportunity, embarrassment, compensation for disability, loss of future income—you must rely on judgment born of experience. There are no positive, definite standards. You are not helpless, however. There are a few guidelines:

1. Verdicts Set the Standards for Settlements.

As a general rule no one is going to pay more in a settlement than the highest verdict that has been obtained in your area in a similar case. That is one place to start your search. Court personnel freely trade gossip about verdicts, and a good friend on the staff can help you immeasurably in locating the verdicts in cases similar to yours. Look them over, compare the special damages (medical bills, lost wages and the like), the nature of the injury, the liability, and if they are reasonably close to your own case use them as a guide.

2. Settlements Recently Made By Fellow Lawyers Are a Reasonable Guide.

More than once I have had an unusual type of case only to find, on making inquiry, that other lawyers had a case that was close in point and settled it for so-and-so a figure. That helps—provided that lawyer is as good as you are, that the two cases are really comparable, and that there was not some special, novel, factor that brought about his settlement. I call to mind a recent case, widely reported on the television and in newspapers, in which a young steel worker was trapped on a girder of a bridge that was being demolished. TV cameras focused on him as he screamed and writhed in pain while his fellow workers worked with terrible slowness to free him for fear the whole structure would collapse, killing them all. Finally an orthopedic surgeon had to be summoned who, right on the girder, in full view of all, and administering a minimal amount of anesthetic, had to cut off the leg. That case eventually settled for an enormous sum, but it hardly stands for a standard by which to measure the value of all "leg off" cases. It's that kind of thing you have to beware of when talking with your friend.

Likewise, in an assumpsit case, you can hardly use for comparison a similar case in which the defendant corporation burned records to avoid discovery, bribed employees to lie, and sent a key officer-witness to Europe to avoid the taking of his deposition or appearance at trial. Settlement in such a case should be at the rate of 100 percent of value and it cannot be used as a standard.

But your brethren at the Bar have been through most of the cases that may be new to you and dutiful inquiry will enable you to turn up enough cases to provide an emerging pattern to help you.

If you are a defense attorney, the problem of evaluation is a little easier since your insurance company or corporate client will have both statistics and a company policy to assist you. You aren't left to grope your way quite as much as Plaintiff's attorney is required to do. Quite likely an opinion letter will have been written and a reserve established so that you already have guidelines to assist you in settlement. Thereafter it is a matter of evaluating the changes developed during the discovery process and then arriving at a more up-to-date settlement range. But still novel and unusual cases will come along from time to time, and you too will be thrust in the position of searching for a verdict in a comparable case or "sounding out" your contemporaries about their settlements, if any, in similar situations.

3. Utilize the Various Books and Guides Found in Every Law Library.

There are many books on the subject of settlement that should be perused if you have an especially troublesome problem. In addition, there is one set of handbooks that I have found to be especially helpful in giving general guidelines. That series is

> Personal Injury Valuation Handbooks
> by Jury Verdict Research, Inc.
> Caxton Building
> Cleveland, Ohio 44115

This series of handbooks divides its review into sections dealing with verdicts for all kinds of specific injuries and also analyzes verdicts from the point of view of different liability situations. For example, on the injury side the handbooks will take a "below-knee amputation," and give you a Mid-point Range, Probability Range, Verdict Range and Average Value, followed by references to specific cases. On the liability side they will cite "Medical Malpractice—Fracture Treatment," and in a brief discussion give the total number of cases reviewed, the percent that were Plaintiff's verdicts, and again, a reference to some specific case examples. It's a good series and I recommend that you look at it for help in evaluating your case.

Unfortunately, however, there is no book or manual that can give you specific help to answer the twin questions: "What is my case worth?" and "What shall I offer (or demand)?" You can only review the verdicts, consult with your acquaintances and friends, study your case and make adjustments in the figures you learn of, as needed, and then, based on your own experience, arrive at a settlement range that you deem fair and reasonable.

IV. WORK WITH OPPOSING COUNSEL

Please notice the use of the word "with" in the title above. It's a common mistake to treat opposing counsel almost like an enemy—as if he or she was *personally* paying the money (or receiving it) and *deliberately* obstructing your honorable efforts to secure a just settlement of the case. While this may be a slight exaggeration of the true state of affairs, it is correct that many attorneys enter into settlement negotiations with a chip on their shoulder, daring the other side to knock it off. All these lawyers get is a fight—not a settlement.

Instead, actively strive to work with your adversary. He or she can help you by pointing out the problems he or she has in dealing with the client, or areas in which you will need additional proof, or doubts that have been expressed about the integrity of your principal witness, or the state of the law. Once you recognize these matters as problems, you can arrange to have on hand the manner of resolving them quickly. Yet you would never have known of these obstacles if opposing counsel was offended by your attitude and kept still. And don't forget that very often your adversary has a good deal of discretion given him by his client. He can use that discretion in a friendly or a hostile manner, to help you or hurt you. Why invite trouble? Go out of your way to work *with* the attorney on the other side and you can accomplish wonders. It's still true that honey gets more bees than vinegar.

There are several specific areas in which Defense attorneys usually need some help:

1. Documentation of a Plaintiff's Claims.

The Defendants always need proof—preferably of a documentary nature—of various aspects of a Plaintiff's claim, but principally in the area of damages.

Thus, if a Plaintiff claims that he or she was working at a second job, received payment in cash, and is demanding this loss as part of his or her damages, you will have to do more than rely on Plaintiff's bare assertion of that fact. The Defendant, legitimately, will want to see income tax returns and/or a statement from the employer regarding hours worked and payments made.

As another example, while medical and hospital bills are easily and routinely procured, payments for household services—a legitimate claim—are usually not made on the basis of a written contract and are often paid in cash. Here too, a statement will be needed that the work was done and the payments made.

Large corporations frequently get into violent disputes—especially when working on a "cost plus fixed fee" basis—as to the legitimacy of the claimed "cost," or if on a "time and materials" contract, as to the amount of time that was necessary and the true cost of the materials. While representing a steel fabricating company in a claim against a major construction company I had to be amused as the respective teams of accountants, engineers and managers took off their coats, sat at a long table, and went at it one day—and the whole fight was over the bills for time and materials from the fabricator: whether the "time" was inflated, and whether the costs for material from the sub-contractors were correct. If my client had not had detailed statements, financial records and affidavits, the case would never have settled—but we did and it did.

Your opponent wants proof, not mere verbal assertion of fact, regarding damages. Your job is to see to it that he, or she, gets what is needed.

2. The Current State of the Law in Novel Cases.

If plaintiff is proceeding on the basis of some esoteric, novel, or even slightly unusual theory of law it is only reasonable, when defense counsel expresses doubts, to provide him or her with a memo explaining why the theory is justified. To illustrate, the City of Pittsburgh owns a very steep hillside covered with trees and underbrush—and rocks. A major road runs along this hillside, and on the day in question as a taxicab proceeded up the hill a large rock rolled down, came through the windshield, and injured the passenger. The City took the position that this incident was a natural event over which it had no control and for which it was not responsible, even though it had happened before. Essentially the position was that the rocks could not be controlled and that the only alternative was to shut down the road, which it felt the law did not require.

This was certainly not a routine case and defense counsel was impressed with the logic of his position and felt no need for legal research. Since he wouldn't to it, I had to. Lo and behold—I found that there is authority that if a municipality cannot control natural forces that endanger a road it has the duty to close the road rather than subject its citizens to known dangers while using it. A short brief to that effect was sufficient to convince both the defense attorney and the city fathers, and the case was settled.

There are a lot of things like that which can be resolved if you will do the research, write a Brief or memo, and use it to convince the other side that liability exists. I recall a case in which two automobiles collided head-on at night on an isolated country road, killing both drivers. The only witness was a passenger who died soon after, but not before giving a brief statement to a driver of a car who arrived at the scene sometime later. The issue was whether the statement constituted a Dying Declaration exception to the Hearsay Rule. The burden was clearly on Plaintiff's counsel to satisfy the Defendant that it did, and a good brief on the subject accomplished that purpose.

In another case you might be confronted with the issue of whether an agent was within or without the scope of his authority when he performed some unusual act. If you will do the research to satisfy the Defendant that the person was acting within his delegated authority, the case may settle; if you won't do the work, now, it will not be settled. At the same time remember that the issue will remain to haunt you and will still be there at trial time. Then you will most certainly have to brief it for the Court. Why wait? If that is a central issue in the lawsuit let the Defendant know, early in the case, that you have a solid position and settle the case!

Don't permit yourself to be either too proud or too lazy to do a little research and brief writing for the opposition. It's in your best interest to do so.

3. Letting Your Opponent Have Your Items of Proof as to Liability.

When some attorneys have an item of evidence that represents a key to the liability side of the case, they tend to clutch it to their chests as though they had just lifted the Hope diamond from the Smithsonian and you literally have to pry it from them, if you get it at all. Their fear is that if the opposition knows of it they (the opposition) will connive to destroy its effectiveness or utility. That attitude is absurd. To begin with, under current discovery rules the evidence can be uncovered one way or another, and second, most lawyers aren't in the "conniving" business. If the evidence is as damning as one thinks it is, the other side will want to settle—not lie or evade. However, they have to see it before they can acknowledge that it is damning; and if you don't show it to them they can never make a judgment in the matter. That's why it is so silly and self-defeating to "hide" evidence. Give it to your opponent so that he or she can see for himself or herself that your case is strong; the next topic for conversation will be the subject of settlement.

One sad but hilarious example of the benefits of this approach involved a case where a young child received a bicycle for a birthday present. While riding it that day the brakes failed, and the child was struck by a car and injured. The father was a mechanical engineer who assured me that the brakes were poorly designed and inoperative, but he adamantly refused to permit the Defendant's experts to see the bike. That was THE EXHIBIT, THE PROOF, and no one could see it. In due course of time I persuaded him that he was wrong and arranged a time for an inspection, and on the day appointed the defense attorney and the expert showed up and examined the bike in Plaintiff's garage. The expert pronounced the brakes sound over my client's howling objections. The defense attorney—a husky young man—asked my permission to ride the bike and I assented. He circled the garage once and flew down the steep driveway—directly into the path of an oncoming car. He just barely shot past it as we all raced to the street. Ashen-faced, he pushed the bike back to us and, glaring at his expert, said to me: "Let's settle this case. The goddamned brakes don't work!"

So much for keeping evidence from the other side.

Seriously, if you have evidence that clinches the case, let your opponent have it. If it is as sound and relevant as you think it is the other attorney will appreciate the poor position he or she is in and will want to settle the case.

4. Evaluating a Difficult Case.

This is one more area in which your assistance might be helpful to the other side. It is possible that you have the kind of case in which the normal guidelines and standards are inapplicable. If you have scouted around and learned of settlements or verdicts by other attorneys—perhaps in neighboring jurisdictions—don't keep them under your hat. Share the information with defense counsel so that he or she knows that there is exposure and that your demand was not wholly a product of whimsy and imagination.

If you have friends in the Legislature and have based your case on a bill that is about to become Law, or has just been passed, you might as well tell the defense attorney instead of having him or her floundering around wondering about the basis of your claim. They have as much trouble keeping up with the changes in the law as you do, and any help you can give in that regard will be appreciated.

Finally, if there is some significant aspect to either side of a case that lifts it out of the normal situation, that should be specifically called to the attention of Defense counsel so that he or she can take it into consideration. For example, you may have a case involving a serious injury to a young child who is being attended to by its mother, and predictably, this will continue. Now if the mother should develop a tumor which both limits her life expectancy and requires serious medical treatment for her, then the claim for damages on behalf of the child can change abruptly and significantly.

There can be other events such as this which suddenly appear and significantly change the ordinary appraisal of a case. When they do occur be certain that the other side is informed so that they can understand your evaluation of the case.

5. Giving the Other Attorney the Documentary Information He Needs.

I have often heard attorneys express their strong feelings that they will not turn over to their opposing counsel various documents that he or she wants. Usually they refer to experts' reports, letters from attending physicians, income tax returns, statistical analysis and other important data. This always seemed strange to me; if the other attorney is to be kept in the dark about vital information pertaining to the case, how will he or she ever be in a position to evaluate it for settlement purposes? The answer is obvious—he or she can't do it. To refuse to divulge pertinent information is simply to cut off your nose to spite your face. It's ridiculous. If parties are seriously interested in settling a case and a Plaintiff's attorney has experts' reports that clearly point to liability on the part of the defendant, he should run—not walk—to get them into the hands of the defense attorney. That is exactly the kind of information your opponent must have to evaluate the case himself and to discuss it intelligently with his client. It's in your best interest to show your adversary counsel that you do have a strong case. You do that best by overwhelming him or her with factual data. So, let your emphasis be, not on withholding significant data, but on divulging it— promptly. The more your opponent knows, the more realistic he or she will be in settlement negotiations.

KNOW YOUR OPPONENT—WHAT KIND OF PERSON IS HE, OR SHE?

It is trite, but necessary, to mention that everyone has a distinct personality and a particular way of doing things. Since, to effect a settlement, you have to reach an agreement with the other lawyer, go out of your way to learn what kind of person he or she is and how that person conducts his or her business. If that lawyer is a "detail person," give him or her a detailed analysis of the case; if he or she is proud of being a scholar, prepare a little brief; if longwinded talk is their forte, be prepared to spend an afternoon with them. You're trying to convince the other attorney and you must adjust to his or her foibles. There are other things you have to bear in mind:

1. Does this lawyer speak with authority? If you reach an agreement with him or her, can he or she produce?

2. Is this a person who will reach an understanding with you and then come back later with a tale of woe asking that you increase (or lower) the agreed-upon figure?

3. Will this attorney take the time to go through the facts and the proofs with you?

4. Will this attorney be honest in appraising the facts with you? Or is he or she one of those persons who won't even acknowledge the identity of the Plaintiff and Defendant?

5. Does this lawyer know the case well enough to debate its virtues and vices with you?

These are some of the things you have to learn before you meet to discuss settlement. Each type of personality, each varied attitude, can be handled if you just know about it in advance and take the time to figure out how to resolve it.

PREPARE A SMALL BROCHURE OR SYNOPSIS OF YOUR CASE

This is most important for Plaintiff's attorneys. Very often pertinent facts are scattered in a dozen different places in a file. If you consider that most defense attorneys have dozens of files and are quite busy, you will realize that it is both difficult and time-consuming for them to search for and summarize these facts. It helps your cause to do it for them. In addition, when you present them with a little summary of the case it gives them something concrete to pass on to their insurance company or corporate client as a basis for justifying their recommendation for settlement.

Your summary can be detailed if you think it will help—going into your theory of liability and referring to specific evidence you have for each element of your cause of action. Usually, though, you can leave that matter to verbal discussion with the defense attorney. Most often your summary can be directed to biographical details and proofs relating to losses and damages. The following represents just such a summary prepared in a death case for settlement discussion. Attached to it, as exhibits, were letters from the employers verifying the wage record, copies of funeral bills and other last expenses, and copies of the hospital and medical bills.

This was a medical malpractice case in which the decedent died because a nurse in the Intensive Care Unit had, allegedly, prematurely withdrawn an endo-tracheal tube after surgery. The man involved was a retiree who, although on a pension, had secured another job which provided him with a little activity and income. The liability side of the case was the subject of several conferences but the damages aspects were pretty well covered by this summary.

SUMMARY

JOHN P. JONES

BIRTHDATE: 2-13-12
DATE OF DEATH: 6-1-80
AGE: 68

LIFE EXPECTANCY: 13.4 years

RETIRED J&L—11-2-71—See Exhibit 1.
PENSION—$388.67—Subject to Increases of a Non-Predeterminal
     nature
1979—$4,664.04 Total Pension Paid

II. *WORKED FOR COMMONWEALTH OF PA.*—See Exhibit 2.
Began—10-29-71
Position—Administrative Assistant I—Inheritance Tax Office
   $1,332.00/mo.

EARNINGS

1976-$13,101.23	1979-$16,862.55
1977-$13,429.37	1980-$ 7,392.60

No Compulsory Retirement

III. ESTIMATED RECOVERY-
Work: $17,000.00 x 7 years $119,000.00
Pension: $4,700.00 x 13.4 years 62,980.00
              TOTAL$181,980.00

IV. FUNERAL, BURIAL AND OTHER LAST EXPENSES—See Exhibit 3.

              TOTAL $7,182.07

V. MEDICAL EXPENSES—See Exhibit 4.

              TOTAL $8,868.17

TOTAL LOSS OF EARNINGS OF MR. JONES......$181,980.00
TOTAL EXPENSES...............................$ 16,050.24
LOSS OF CONSORTIUM OF MRS. JONES
For 13.4 years ....???

This made a nice package for the benefit of both defense counsel and the claims persons at the insurance company. Since the case was settled for a fair sum, this little summary obviously did some good. At least there was no argument about these various elements of damage.

MAKE A SENSIBLE, REALISTIC OFFER OR DEMAND

There are few things more irritating than to have a case that truly has a value of, let us say, $50,000.00 and to receive an offer of $7,500.00, unless it's one that has a value of $2,500.00 and the demand is $100,000.00. Ridiculous offers and demands are the cause of death of more settlement negotiations than any other reason. You've seen this sort of thing happen. The case plods along to a trial date, and lo and behold—the one settles for $47,500.00 and the other for $2,000.00. Chat some day with a trial judge and he will tell you, wearily, story after story like this. Most of the time the problem lies with inexperience on the part of counsel, but once in awhile it is caused by the deliberate policy of some insurance company or the intransigence of a stubborn client.

Insofar as it is within your power don't play this game. Certainly it is expected that Plaintiff's attorneys will start high and then come down just as defense attorneys start low and come up. But there are sensible parameters to this bargaining called for by the facts of the case. I knew a wonderful Federal Judge who always had fun with Plaintiff's attorneys during his inevitable settlement conferences by asking:

> "What is your demand?" [Then]
> "What do you really want?" [Then]
> "Now, what will you take?"

It was good-natured fun until one got clearly out of line, then hell broke loose. He was even-handed—many a defense attorney made hurried calls to his client, from Chambers, with an Order from the Judge as to what the offer was going to be! This Judge had a settlement rate of about 95 percent and they were fair, equitable settlements.

So appraise your case realistically, allow a little room for bargaining, and give a demand or an offer that can lead to settlement and accomplish the purpose of the meeting.

KEEP AFTER THE OTHER ATTORNEY

It's rare to be able to settle a case in one meeting. Afterward each side will want to think about the negotiations, look again at the evidence and confer with their respective clients. At the same time remember the old adage, "Out of sight, out of mind." It's too easy to dictate a letter after the conference, set the file aside, and forget about it. That won't do. It's a little like making fudge: somebody has to go to the stove and stir it from time to time or it turns bad. You have to do that with settlements. If there has been no word from the other attorney in two or three weeks you will have to call and inquire as to what is happening. Frequently you will learn that he forgot to send a letter or someone was out of town the last time he called and he just forgot to try again. This may go on several times—that's normal—but if you will just be persistent it will pay off. There may be one last go-round of bargaining and then the case is settled. It's hard work, but it's worth it.

DON'T TRY TO DO THE IMPOSSIBLE; SOME CASES CAN NOT BE SETTLED

There is an old cliché that "politics is the art of the possible." It's a good saying and it implies that, from time to time, certain things simply can't be done. That is certainly true of settlements. Try as you might there are some cases that can't be settled. Don't fight it. With your discovery completed, the case is in the best possible posture for a trial, so simply set it aside until it is called.

There are several reasons for a failure in settlement negotiations. The principal one is an unrealistic demand or offer on the part of the attorneys. If the culpable party adamantly refuses to reconsider his or her position the settlement talks collapse. A second common explanation is an unreasonable attitude on the part of the client. As I mentioned before, emotions are a part of every lawsuit and sometimes they blind the client to reality. The client simply refuses to believe a certain witness is valueless or that the law prohibits him or her from using certain evidence. When you're faced with this kind of intransigence there is nothing else to do but to try the case and, as it unfolds in Court, hope that your client will accept the fact that things are not as he or she wants or believes them to be. Unfortunately, by that time any hope of a reasonably good settlement will be gone.

In addition to these reasons for failure to negotiate a fair settlement, one must know that some insurance companies and corporations have an established policy of not negotiating in good faith, of waiting to the bitter end before offering a fair amount in settlement. Plaintiff's attorneys will talk of being "nickled and dimed to death" as the multiple offers are made in small, increasing increments. From this comes the saying that "the best settlements are made on the courthouse steps." By experience, and friendly talks with the other lawyers, you will learn which companies these are and you will have to react accordingly. Fortunately that approach has pretty much gone out of style due to criticism from scholars and the public, pressure from the Bench, changes in the Rules of Procedure, and, probably, sound business practices.

Finally we have the Plaintiff's attorney who will not give up his or her gambling "go for broke" attitude until the day of trial when he or she suddenly realizes he or she is bluffing no one—or the defense attorney who hangs on to the bitter end because he is being paid an hourly fee and the longer he hangs onto a case the more money he makes. The reputation of these people is known in your community, and when you come up against them all you can do is accept them for what they are and forget about settlement.

GUIDELINES FOR NEGOTIATING
A GOOD SETTLEMENT

1. Determine a reasonable settlement range.

   a) Check verdicts in similar cases.
   b) Make inquiry about settlements from your friends.
   c) Check books and manuals in the library.

2. Make a realistic offer or demand.

3. Work with—not against—opposing counsel.

4. Know the kind of person you are dealing with.

5. Give the other attorney the data he needs.

6. Prepare a brochure or synopsis of the case—especially relating to damages and losses.

7. Bargain on a face-to-face basis; avoid telephone conferences.

8. Keep after the other attorney; don't let the negotiations get cold.

Index

A